The Inspiring Teacher

Making a Positive Difference

In

Students' Lives

Bob Sullo

Funderstanding LLC
New Jersey

The Inspiring Teacher
Copyright 2013 Bob Sullo

ISBN 10: 0985680695
ISBN 13: 978-0-9856806-9-5

ADVISORY PANEL

James Duggins
Professor of Education
San Francisco State University
San Francisco, California

Arlene Lewis Dykes
Third Grade Teacher
Disnard Elementary School
Claremont, New Hampshire

Melissa W. Earnest
Teacher Caldwell County High School
Princeton, Kentucky

Thomas Ousley
Director of Attendance
Jennings School District
Jennings, Missouri

Rosalind Lucille Yee
Reading Specialist
Prince George's County School System
Annapolis, Maryland

The word education comes from the Latin educare, "to draw out."
The word inspire is derived from the Latin inspirare, "to breathe into."
The Inspiring Teacher will help you breathe life into students and
draw out their full potential to learn.

The journey is worthwhile because teachers who inspire their students
live purposefully, make a meaningful contribution to the world, and experience profound personal and professional satisfaction.

This book is for my parents, Blase and Evelyn Sullo.

Every child should be so lucky.

TABLE OF CONTENTS

Foreword

I cannot imagine any teachers opening this book without having some desire to improve themselves. In essence that is what this book is about, becoming a more effective teacher. A central message of the author is that, to be effective, the teacher needs to be inspiring and he elaborates on how to achieve this throughout the text.

These pages will help educators revisit the values that led them to become teachers in the first place and will help them check the effectiveness of their current approach. But that is not all. *The Inspiring Teacher* will invite the reader to consider a very new approach to teaching and learning and will offer many practical tips along the way.

A word of caution! Do not expect these ideas to sit comfortably in the context of traditional teaching. Neither do they present an easy solution to the many difficulties facing the teachers of today. There are no easy quick-fixes. However, an approach based on a sound psychological theory has the best chance of success. The alternative is to continue as we have always done with the same frustrations and problems of the past, using methods of external control that impede learning and alienate students.

The book is not simply a collection of isolated tips. Instead, it presents a solid theory on which these tips are based. I refer to William Glasser's Choice Theory psychology. Bob Sullo presents a precise and accurate summary of this new way of understanding human behaviour. In turn this will help teachers better comprehend their students and will help them reappraise the teaching methods they use in the classroom.

Bob also offers a selection of useful psychological analyses of teenage development, ideas that will help educators see their students in a totally different light, making sense of some of the mysterious ways of adolescents.

A constant theme throughout the book is the simple but oft-forgotten message that the most needy kids need us most. What tends to have been missing in the formation of teachers is a good understanding of these children and of ways to interact effectively with them. *The Inspiring Teacher* addresses this issue very well.

Around the world there are schools that have adopted Choice Theory as a general school approach with amazing outcomes in terms of the wellbeing of students and staff, impressive state examination results and a most welcome reduction in discipline problems. However, many teachers who welcome the Choice Theory approach do not have the luxury of a supportive administration and staff. For them I believe it is helpful to identify one or more colleagues who are open to these ideas and to study this book together, one chapter at a time, teasing out the ideas and recommendations, trying them out and fine-tuning the approach.

Bob Sullo writes with a deep conviction grounded in years of experience in the classroom. In these pages he shares both his experience and his passion with the reader. The new ideas might even keep you awake at night ... but it will be worth it!

Brian Lennon
Chairperson, William Glasser International

Acknowledgments

Like every student who has experienced some success, I have been helped by many inspiring teachers. With apologies to those I have unintentionally forgotten, I want to acknowledge the following very special people: my parents, Mrs. Cronin (Weymouth Public Schools), Miss Mahoney (Weymouth Public Schools), Mr. Lewis (Weymouth Public Schools), Mr. Emerson (Weymouth Public Schools), Mr. Dwyer (Weymouth Public Schools), Dr. Callahan (Holy Cross College), Dr. Savage (Boston College), Dr. Kelly (Boston College), Dr. Glasser (The William Glasser Institute), and Eric Jensen.

Thanks, too, to my colleagues in the field of education, both those with whom I worked in the public school system in Plymouth, Massachusetts, and those I've met in training workshops around the world. They've told me of their struggles and shared their successes. I've met beginning teachers who bring energy and freshness to the classroom. I've worked with experienced teachers who maintain their enthusiasm and are energized by the knowledge that what they do every day matters tremendously. Their willingness to share has helped me be a more competent educator.

Thanks to everyone at the NEA Professional Library who helped make *The Inspiring Teacher* a reality and allowed it to be converted to this new format.

A special thanks to Paul Kondo and Sam Lee for their expert help in converting the latest version of *The Inspiring Teacher* to print. As exciting as it was to create an e-book version of *The Inspiring Teacher,* I received numerous requests from educators who still find comfort and familiarity in having a "real" book in their hands. Paul and Sam listened to those requests and ensured that readers can now enjoy *The Inspiring Teacher* in their preferred format.

As always, I am most appreciative to my wife Laurie who graciously and lovingly excuses me when I get "lost" in a new writing project. Her support for my work is unconditional.

Finally, thanks to Eric Cohen of Funderstanding. Eric and I have worked together for the past several years and engaged in a number of thoughtful and enjoyable conversations. It has come to the point where I can almost forgive him for being a New York Giants fan. Eric's dedication to educators, kids, and parents is impressive, genuine, and reflected in what he brings to Funderstanding.com. It has been a pleasure to collaborate on this project and I look forward to our next adventure.

Invitation

Why Read *The Inspiring Teacher?*

Let's start with an obvious question: "Who should read *The Inspiring Teacher?*" Fair enough question. In putting together this newly revised edition, I had three specific groups in mind.

The Inspiring Teacher is for every teacher and teacher in training who wants more than just a job. It is for those who want to create rich, meaningful professional identities. It is for those who want to positively impact the lives of their students. It is for those who are determined to make a difference. *The Inspiring Teacher* is also for every parent who wants their kids to internalize important values and behave responsibly even when no one is watching and there is no promise of a "Student of the Month" award or a "Good Boy/Good Girl" shouted in their direction.

If you're in at least one of these groups, *The Inspiring Teacher* is for you. Let me elaborate:

Teachers

In addition to classroom teachers, I'm writing with counselors, psychologists, paraprofessionals, school leaders, and all support staff in mind. In short, everyone who works in a school and wants kids to learn as much as possible and grow into happy, healthy, responsible adults.

Noble intentions are a nice place to start, but good intentions aren't enough. You need specific skills and information. *The Inspiring Teacher* will increase your ability to:

- Understand what drives behavior, how children develop, and what is typical behavior at various stages of development.
- Structure classrooms so that students learn most easily and efficiently.
- Collaborate effectively with colleagues.
- Engage parents and create the positive alliances with them.
- Resolve conflict effectively and respectfully.
- Manage time wisely, even with the increasing demands you face each year – think No Child Left Behind, AYP, Common Core Curriculum, State and National Standards, etc.
- Adapt as new information and new technology impact what we know about best practices in education.
- Inspire students rather than trying to control and manage them.
- Re-claim your professional identity. Most teachers entered the profession because they love kids and learning. Too many tell me they feel battered and beaten down. *The Inspiring Teacher* will remind you why you became a teacher in the first place: to be an inspiration. To make a positive difference. To be a person who matters.

Teachers In Training

Pre-service teachers are better prepared than ever in two key areas: curriculum and instructional practices. But we continue to train new teachers how to "motivate" kids and emphasize classroom management and control. Well-respected educational sites have countless discussion groups dedicated to such topics as "What's the Best Classroom Management Advice You've Gotten."

From my perspective, current postings continue to emphasize external control. Sure, there is some conversation about how to collaborate with kids and inspire them to learn, but it's still essentially about how to keep them in line.

If you are planning to become a teacher (or even thinking about the possibility), I want to expose you to a whole new way of understanding student motivation. I don't even care if you disagree with some of what I suggest. Teachers in training deserve a chance to get involved in serious conversation about motivation and the importance of inspiring our kids. We have no shortage of serviceable teachers. We have a critical shortage of inspirational teachers. When we shift how we approach students and organize schools and classrooms, student learning and achievement will increase. As long as we continue down the "control and manage" road, we'll have teachers creating beautifully designed lessons and a flat-out elegant curriculum while the shameful drop-out rate continues unabated. *The Inspiring Teacher* will serve as a springboard for fruitful discussion that will equip pre-service teachers with greater skills to engage and inspire their students. My hope is that every teacher preparation program offers pre-service teachers a chance to read this book, argue about it, discuss it, and deeply consider how to inspire the kids they will encounter when they join the profession. We owe it not only to students, but also to the next generation of teachers.

Parents

Even if you aren't an educator, if you are a parent of a child in school there is much in *The Inspiring Teacher* for you. I don't want to descend into cliché, but it's true that parents are the first teachers. You'll be better able to do your job as a parent when you better understand motivation. (Note: It's way more than rewards and punishments.) And everything written in *The Inspiring Teacher* can be applied to other situations, including parenting.

Too many parents have behavior charts on the refrigerator, give their kids tangible rewards for good behavior and academic achievement, and sign home-school communication notebooks, only to discover that their kids still haven't internalized important behaviors and values. If you want your kids to behave appropriately and do their best in school because it's the right thing to do and not because they're "getting something," *The Inspiring Teacher* is worth your time.

Introduction

I have spent my entire professional life in education. I don't know about other professions, but educators sure like to complain! With increasing demands that often seem to have more to do with filling out forms and keeping the bean counters happy, rather than helping kids grow and develop into happy, competent, responsible adults, there's always something to complain about. Still, most teachers would echo the words of a friend of mine, a veteran educator who said to me some years ago, "Sure, there's more stress than there used to be and I may not make a lot of money, but I make something more important. I make a difference in the lives of my students. That's something that will never be taken away from good teachers."

Education really is a noble profession. Every day we have a chance to make a positive difference in the lives of our students. Years ago, I read a book by Dan Millman called *No Ordinary Moments* (1992). While it had nothing to do with teaching, the title beautifully captures the magic of education. It doesn't matter if I have taught the same concept to five different classes for the past twenty-whatever years. It's new to the kids and every moment – yes, even those "been there...done that" moments – could very well be something they'll remember forever. Because what we do impacts the future, our lives are full of meaning and purpose.

I do lots of staff development for schools. It's not unusual for a teacher to ask, "Do you think what I'm doing makes any difference?" My answer is always the same: "The question is not whether you make a difference – you do! The question is 'What kind of difference do you want to make?'" Teachers often have no idea

idea what a difference they make in the lives of their students. But every once in a while, a teacher is lucky enough find out just how much they matter. Here's one example:

Some years ago, I attended a ceremony recognizing the academic achievement of some students in the middle school where I worked. It was our tradition to invite a high school student to speak at the event, and the speaker was a senior who was planning to major in Spanish in college the next year. "I started learning Spanish here in middle school with Mrs. Palladino. She wasn't the easiest teacher I had but because of her, I've decided this is what I want to study in college. I've had a number of good teachers, but she really challenged me and inspired me." Sentiments like these, even when they aren't uttered at a public event, make teaching much more than just a job.

In classrooms every day, teachers come face-to-face with youngsters who quite literally will create the future. We may not know what the future will bring and what our students will ultimately become, but inspiring teachers know their job is to help each of their students be the best they can be and experience the joy of learning. Each student has the capacity to be inspired and each teacher has the potential to inspire the next great scientist, musician, entrepreneur, artist, scholar, author, entertainer, doctor, or.... teacher.

Beyond the mandates and inconveniences, think of what transpires in our classrooms. We unlock hearts and minds. We open eyes. We inspire greatness in our students.

Don't be discouraged by the obstacles. When all is said and done, the magic of teaching takes place in the interaction between you and your students. No test, no legislation, no policy can ever deny you the ability to inspire your students.

How This Book Is Organized

The Inspiring Teacher is divided into Part I – Foundation, and Part II – Application. Part I provides an overview of motivation, brain-based learning, and developmental issues. Even if theory isn't your cup of tea, familiarity with the concepts presented in Part I will enable you to take full advantage of the strategies offered later in the book. I've never been a fan of the "1000 Proven Strategies," cookie-cutter, cookbook approach to education. A solid theory is essential to apply strategies effectively and elegantly. I won't cave into the demand to "just tell us what to do." Instead, I'll give you enough foundation in Part I so you can discover the best way to apply what's presented in later chapters. Part II moves from knowledge to application, considers the qualities of an inspiring teacher, addresses how to inspire students and colleagues, and suggests how to build positive alliances with parents. It also includes chapters on conflict management and time management.

Each chapter of *The Inspiring Teacher* ends with a section inviting you to "Reflect, Personalize, and Implement" what has been learned. Why? It is necessary to *reflect* on newly acquired information to internalize it – to "own" it. Research suggests that the most effective professional development programs invite teachers to *personalize* what they have learned by relating it to what they experience every day (Sparks & Hirsh 1997). Since unapplied knowledge is of little value, I will invite you to identify how you will *implement* what you have learned in each chapter. If you choose to use *The Inspiring Teacher* as I recommend, it will help you enhance your skills and put your knowledge to work every day.

Giving Thanks

Before you delve into Chapter 1, take a moment to remember those who inspired you. They may have been classroom teachers, coaches, advisers, paraprofessionals, counselors, administrative staff, or administrators. It might have been years later when it dawned on you just how inspirational they had been and how much they had contributed to your growth and development. Give each of them the heartfelt thanks they deserve. And remember that you, too, can give the same gift to your students. You can be an inspiring teacher that makes a positive difference in the lives of your students.

PART I

FOUNDATION

CHAPTER 1

Motivation: The Inside Story

Learning may be natural, but the acquisition of academic skills - school learning - is not. It requires motivation. How do we become motivated to learn what is asked of us in school? Contrary to conventional wisdom, it is impossible for one person to motivate another. As you will discover in this chapter, motivation always comes from the inside.

The most prevalent theory of motivation in the world is external control psychology. Derived primarily from the work of John Watson and B.F. Skinner, external control psychology can be summed up as follows: human behavior is a response to outside stimuli. When people are rewarded or reinforced for a particular behavior, they are more likely to repeat that behavior. When people are punished for a particular behavior, they are less likely to engage in it again.

External control psychology appeals to many. First, it is a simple, "common sense" explanation of behavior and motivation. It takes complex, multifaceted human beings and reduces them to simple, reactive creatures who can be controlled by rewards and punishments. Second, external control psychology is particularly attractive to those who seek to control others. It claims that humans are naturally malleable. We only need to develop an effective system of rewards and punishments and we can get others to do our bidding.

Despite its continued prevalence, external control psychology is fundamentally flawed and never inspires people to do their best. We are much more complex than external control psychology proponents would have us believe. We are not simple, reactive creatures capable of being programmed like robots. In fact, because we have a drive to be autonomous, any attempt – however well intentioned – to shape our behavior invites defiance. People generally do not accept external control, even when it is allegedly for their benefit.

I don't want to suggest that external control psychology never works. It can be effective when the goal is compliance rather than quality. If all I want is for you to perform a simple task, one without gradations of quality, I might entice you with a reward or create enough fear with the threat of punishment that I get you to do what I desire, at least short-term. The cost, however, is great. Research strongly suggests that external rewards decrease internal motivation (Amabile 1989). Is that what you want for your students? Your own kids? Moreover, I contend that you are internally motivated even in the example just cited. You are driven by what *you* want: the reward I am offering or the avoidance of punishment. That's dramatically different from suggesting that I motivated you to learn.

We generally don't look for simple compliance in our classrooms. We want the best work a student can produce. As long as we rely on approaches based on external control, we will be no more successful than we have been until now. In short, external control psychology has taken us as far as it can. It is an orientation whose application may lead to compliance but it will never inspire quality.

To illustrate, consider how this "carrot and stick" approach is typically used when assigning and evaluating homework. Students typically are rewarded with check marks when they do homework and they are punished with low grades and a loss of credit when they don't. Relying on the carrot and stick approach of external control, we have many compliant students. Lots of homework gets done. On the surface, this seems reasonable.

Unfortunately, much of the homework that is completed is devoid of quality. Teachers frequently give full credit for work that is horrifyingly inadequate simply because it has been done. Are you satisfied with this result? Do you want compliance or do you want to inspire students to engage in meaningful, rigorous work?

Despite the lingering fascination with external control psychology and its continued stranglehold on most schools, numerous writers and thinkers have advanced the notion that we are internally driven.

- In *Man's Search for Meaning*, Victor Frankl states, "Man is ultimately self-determining. Man does not simply exist but always decides what his existence will be, what he will become in the next moment" (1959, 133).

- William Powers writes, "People control their own experiences. The only way you can truly force them to behave as you wish is through the threat or actuality of overwhelmingly superior physical force – and even that is only a temporary solution" (1998, 122).

- Alfie Kohn adds, "No artificial incentive can match the power of intrinsic motivation" (1993, 68).

- Reporting on the Self-Determination Theory of noted University of Rochester scholars Edward Deci and Richard Ryan, author Daniel Pink states, "They have produced hundreds of research papers, most of which point to the same conclusion. Human beings have an innate drive to be autonomous, self-determined, and connected to one another. And when that drive is liberated, people achieve more and live richer lives" (2009, 73).

- William Glasser, M.D., an acknowledged leader in the field of internal control psychology, states, "What happens outside of us has a lot to do with what we choose to do, but the outside event does not cause our behavior. What we get, and all we ever get from the outside is information; how we choose to act on that information is up to us" (1990, 41).

Education continues to be dominated by the practice of external control psychology, an approach that provides little more than simple, short-term compliance. That may have been adequate in the past, but educators today are being asked to do more. Students will only be successful in an increasingly interdependent world when they are inspired to unleash the drive within and commit to academic achievement. It has never been more important to listen to those who advocate for a model that emphasizes freedom, responsibility, and internal motivation.

While there are various theorists who champion the concepts of internal control and motivation, I highlight choice theory – a comprehensive theory of human behavior developed by William Glasser, M.D. (1998), who has worked closely with schools for a half century. Choice theory respects the complexity of what it means to be human and can be applied in any situation involving interaction.

Those who hope to become inspiring teachers owe it to themselves to become familiar with choice theory. By familiarizing yourself with choice theory, you will be able to move from compliance to quality, and work more effectively with students, parents, and colleagues. It will equip you with the skills to inspire quality work by many more of your students. The remainder of this chapter will familiarize you with several key elements of choice theory.

Choice theory differs from external control psychology in several important ways:

- **Internal motivation.** External control psychology suggests that we are externally motivated by rewards and punishments. Choice theory maintains that we are internally motivated. The outside world provides us with information but does not make us do anything. We are active – not reactive – beings. We are internally driven and choose our behavior.

- **Personal responsibility.** External control psychology suggests that we are "shaped" by external stimuli. If that is true, then being held accountable for our actions is ultimately unfair. We are simply the products of an endless stream of rewards and punishments that have been provided by our parents, teachers, and society. Because choice theory teaches that we choose our behavior and are not "made" to act a certain way by outside forces, it highlights personal responsibility and accountability.

- **Free will.** External control psychology suggests that freedom is an illusion. Practitioners of external control psychology have a view of humanity that denies free will, whereas choice theory teaches that we have free will and are genetically instructed to be free and autonomous.

While I strongly encourage you to develop a thorough understanding of choice theory, three components of choice theory essential to inspiring quality student work are presented here: our basic needs, motivation, and perception.

Basic Needs: Genetic Instructions That Drive Our Behavior

It is widely accepted that we have genetic instructions that impact physical characteristics like height, eye color, and complexion. We also have genetic instructions related to our behavior: instructions to love and connect with others, to seek personal power and competence, to be free and autonomous, to be playful and have fun, and to survive. Our behavior – even behavior we don't understand – is always purposeful, our attempt to follow the instructions written into our genes.

We choose *how* to satisfy the drives we are born with and we are responsible for the choices we make. While I am genetically driven to gain power, I choose whether to seek power in responsible, prosocial ways or if I will gain power irresponsibly by exploiting and hurting others. The fact that we have been born with genetic drives does not absolve us of responsibility for our actions.

These genetic instructions, also called basic needs, are universal. It doesn't matter if you are young or old, male or female, rich or poor. Even though everyone has all these needs, their intensity varies among individuals. Some people are highly social, strongly driven by the need to connect. Others continually seek more competence and personal power. Still others are especially fueled by a need for autonomy, sometimes at great cost, or are always in pursuit of joy and play. And we all know people who would never skydive, bungee jump, play the stock market, or engage in any high-risk behaviors. These people are strongly driven by the need for safety and security (survival). While the intensity of our needs is determined genetically, adults can help kids develop behaviors that allow them to follow their genetic instructions in responsible ways. This is where "nurture" positively impacts "nature."

The Quality World

Our basic needs are non-specific. For example, we are driven to be loving and connected to others, but we are born with no predetermined notion about *how* to connect or *who* to connect with. The same is true for the other basic needs. Nature provides the drive but not the specifics. Over time, we develop highly defined perceptions of those people, things, activities, and values that are the most need-satisfying and important to us. Choice theory calls this our *quality world*. Everything we place in our quality world is connected to one or more of the basic needs.

We all have the same basic needs, but each person's quality world is unique. My quality world, for example, includes my family, my most important beliefs and values, and those activities that are need-satisfying to me. It's unlikely that my wife and our three kids are in your quality world. And some of you may find gardening to be extremely need-satisfying and have that activity in your quality world. Not me. While our basic needs are universal, our quality world reflects our individuality.

We are motivated by, and work hard for, the things and people in our own unique quality world. Because our quality world is a theoretical construct in our head, motivation is internal. A student who values reading and has it in her quality world is motivated to read. A student who has acting in his quality world will be motivated to pursue drama. A student who values money may earn good grades in order to be financially rewarded by her parents – but she is motivated by the money, not by the learning. Inspiring teachers do everything they can to encourage students to build a quality world that includes learning what we are trying to teach, academic achievement, and social responsibility. Beyond that, we help them develop the requisite behaviors to bring those pictures to fruition.

External Control Versus Internal Motivation

Some years ago I attended a meeting about a student who was not doing well in school. The results of an evaluation requested by Tim's parents suggested he had average cognitive ability with no indications of a learning disability.

At the TEAM meeting, we discussed how to help Tim be more successful. One concern was his refusal to do homework. Someone suggested that Tim earn a point each time he completed a homework assignment, regardless of the quality of the homework. Since Tim loved and excelled in hockey, his parents would make playing hockey contingent upon the number of homework points he earned. If he earned enough points, he could play hockey; if he didn't, he would not be allowed to play.

Everyone at the meeting had Tim's welfare in mind. Everyone except me enthusiastically endorsed this common sense, carrot and stick strategy. I was convinced that we would be teaching Tim – through actions, not words – that doing homework was nothing more than a means to something worthwhile (in his case, hockey). Anything that devalues academic work has no place in the repertoire of the inspiring teacher.

Alfie Kohn captured it eloquently when he wrote, "'Do this and you'll get that' makes people focus on the 'that,' not the 'this.'" (1993, 67.) Tim was already plenty focused on hockey. I wanted him to start focusing on being successful in school. Sadly, the

TEAM decided on a strategy that reduced school, working hard, and homework completion to hoops to be jumped through.

How would I have worked with Tim using the ideas of internal control and motivation? I would have asked him why he liked hockey. I'd want him to see me as an ally, someone interested in him and what he cared for, not simply someone who wanted him to conform to my expectations. Discussing hockey with Tim would also give me a sense of what needs were most important to him. This would have been useful in structuring a need-satisfying school experience. I would have then helped Tim appreciate that completing his homework, working to the best of his ability, and fully involving himself in the process of education were worth doing. They are not worth doing in order to play hockey. They are worth doing for their own sake.

In addition to working directly with Tim, I would have taken a hard look at the system rather than just the presenting symptom. Tim was not an aberration. Why do so many students do homework with little pride or ignore it completely? It's simplistic and erroneous to say that students who don't do homework are "lazy" and "unmotivated." If you watched Tim play hockey, you'd know with certainty that he was neither lazy nor unmotivated. Such labels are misleading and do nothing to address the problem. Frequently, the problem is not the student; it's a flawed system.

School Activities That Satisfy Basic Needs

Consider school activities where students routinely work hard. Many students identified as lazy and unmotivated work as hard as anyone else in athletics, drama, and music. What do these activities have in common?

First, students connect with their peers. Even in a sport involving individual competition, such as tennis, players are part of a team and the feeling of belonging is need-satisfying. Students who participate in music or drama feel sufficiently connected to attend long, arduous practices and work hard while there.

Second, these activities help students develop personal power and competence. In competitive athletics, losing is part of the terrain, but skilled coaches help young athletes feel a sense of accomplishment even when they don't win. Athletes want to win, but coaches help students value the development and improvement of skills even in a losing cause. Drama and music performances similarly help students demonstrate power and competence in a healthy, responsible way. Young musicians who master a difficult piece of music, for example, discover that it feels good to work hard and be successful.

Third, students satisfy the need for freedom in extracurricular activities such as athletics, drama, and music precisely because they are typically electives. Voluntary participation significantly changes the experience for many.

Fourth, athletics, drama, and music generally involve a lot of fun and learning. They also require hard work. Although some coaches are tyrants and punitive taskmasters, the irony is that coaches have less need to be punitive because most athletes want to be successful and willingly do what coaches ask to the best of their ability. Classroom teachers would be delighted if their students demonstrated the same level of hard work, commitment, and motivation that is typically seen in athletics, drama, and music.

Teachers in traditional academic classrooms can learn a lot by looking at what happens in athletics, drama, and music. Students identified as lazy and unmotivated will work hard and produce quality when they can meet their needs by exerting maximum effort. Give students in a traditional academic class tasks that are need-satisfying and they will be highly motivated and almost always do their best. If you ask students to do something that is not satisfying to them, they will either defy you or perform only well enough to get you to leave them alone.

Creating a Need-Satisfying Environment

Structure need-satisfying classrooms and students will produce significantly higher quality academic work in a joyful atmosphere. To inspire your students, give students the opportunity to interact appropriately, allowing them to meet the need to connect. Offer them challenges that satisfy the drive for power and competence. *Note*: while it's important to challenge students, be certain that academic demands are not so overwhelming that kids anticipate failure and give up. Follow the positive example seen in athletics and drama, where students with different abilities are challenged to achieve their best, allowing all of them to feel a legitimate sense of power and competence. The same differentiation is essential in an academic classroom. Tomlinson (1999) and others have written eloquently about how to create classrooms where students of varying ability can achieve power and competence.

The Common Core State Standards, curriculum frameworks, and other accountability initiatives drive today's academic agenda. Some argue that it is impossible to cultivate an environment compatible with the drive for freedom because of these demands. I disagree. Creating an environment that is compatible with the need for freedom does not necessarily mean that people do what they want when they want. Schools require structure. Within even the most defined structure, however, teachers can maintain instructional autonomy and provide options to their students so the need for freedom is accommodated. Here's an example:

The Massachusetts state standard for math in grade 6 includes the following: "Describe and compare data sets using the concepts of median, mean, mode, maximum, minimum, and range" (6.D.1). While teachers are obliged to teach to that standard, they retain autonomy in terms of instruction. They may use suggestions provided in the district curriculum, the approved textbook, or relevant data such as student test scores.

Just as teachers can exercise freedom within a prescribed curriculum, they can offer it to their students as well. Standard 6.M.1 of the Massachusetts state standards asks students to identify different ways rectangles can have an area of 24 square centimeters and to show their work. Teachers can allow students to demonstrate their understanding in several ways:

- A student can draw various rectangles and label the dimensions.

- A student can create multiplication problems with the different factors that have a product of 24 square centimeters.

- A student can use colored tiles or use graph paper to construct various rectangles with an area of 24 units representing 24 square centimeters.

Creative teachers don't allow themselves to be stifled by state mandates. There are ways to offer a standardized curriculum while maintaining instructional independence for teachers and options for students.

Because fun is intimately connected to learning, the most inspiring, educationally rich classrooms are enjoyable for students and teachers alike. Build laughter and joy into your lessons. Anything else would be foolish. Can you imagine inspiring kids in a joyless environment? Students might learn some content, but no one would want to pursue more learning. Communicate your passion and enthusiasm for what you are teaching and help students feel excited about the learning they are doing.

I have worked with teachers around the world who intentionally create need-satisfying classrooms. They consistently report that their students do quality work more regularly than before. Have students changed? I don't think so. What is different is that these teachers are creating classrooms that let students meet their needs by engaging in challenging academic work. In a need-satisfying environment, students produce better work and teachers enjoy themselves more.

People value things that are need-satisfying. When we create need-satisfying classrooms, students value school and learning. They appreciate that academic achievement feels good and working hard is worth the effort. When students value school and learning, they are internally motivated to achieve as much as possible and there is a dramatic improvement in the quality of their work. Students will always need the direct instruction, feedback, and coaching that effective teachers provide, but there will be no question about their motivation and willingness to work hard.

Most teachers tell me they would enjoy their jobs more if their students were more motivated. Class size is important, as is cognitive ability. But these and other factors pale in comparison to motivation. Give a good teacher a room full of motivated, eager students, and wonderful things happen regardless of class size and the inherent cognitive abilities of the learners. Give the same teacher a small group of highly intelligent youngsters who have no desire to learn what is being taught, and the job becomes a nightmare. The good news is that all of us – even the most difficult to reach student – is motivated. All the time. It's the way we're wired. We're motivated to meet our needs and attain the pictures in our quality world. Create a need-satisfying classroom and more kids will put working hard and achieving into their quality world. By the way, there's an additional positive outcome: you'll derive more satisfaction from your job!

Gaining Credibility with Students

To inspire your students, you need to be credible. Kids, especially adolescents, naturally wonder why they should listen to you. How you present yourself and your subject matter will go a long way in determining whether students find you credible. It is essential that you are perceived as genuine. If students sense that you are a phony – saying all the "right" things but meaning none of it - they will shut you out. Who can blame them? Once that happens, what you say makes little difference. Conversely, when students believe that you genuinely care about them, want them to be as successful as possible, and will help them achieve as much as possible, they will generally work hard.

If you have valuable information that you'd like to share with your students, be certain they know you care about them. As someone once told me, "They have to know that you care before they care what you know."

Being genuine is necessary, but it is not enough to inspire your students. They must also respect you. Teachers gain the respect of their students when they take their jobs seriously, take their subject seriously, act professionally, treat students with respect, and maintain high academic and behavioral standards. An inspiring teacher is much more than a "nice" teacher. An inspiring teacher is a consummate professional.

Perception

As information is taken in, it passes through three filters (sensory, knowledge, and valuing) before becoming a perception in our brain. Our perception of reality (true or false) ultimately determines how we behave.

Sensory Filter

Information is first processed by our sensory system. For all practical purposes, things in the "real world" don't exist for us until we sense them. Our senses can distort incoming information to some degree. We've all experienced situations where we "heard" or "saw" incorrectly. Our senses, the first gateway in the perception process, can betray us. Hopefully, our senses provide us accurate information as we create our perceptions.

Knowledge Filter

Human beings are meaning-makers. In our attempt to make sense of the world, we screen all incoming information through our knowledge filter. We interpret new information against everything we already know, regardless of how complete or accurate our knowledge is. A student who "knows" that there are nine continents acts on that information even though it is inaccurate.

The information provided in this chapter provides a good example of how our knowledge filter impacts the perceptions we construct. Some of you are familiar with internal control psychology and choice theory. Others are learning about it for the first time. Although the printed words are the same for all readers, each of you brings your past experience and knowledge to the experience and creates a perception influenced by your pre-existing knowledge.

The same process occurs in a classroom. Imagine you are providing direct instruction to the whole class about early America. Students' perceptions vary based on the knowledge they bring to the lesson. A student who has been to a living history museum will perceive your presentation differently from a student who has not had that experience. Years ago I sat next to a woman on a plane who had just been to Egypt with her grandson, a sixth grade student. Among other things, they had seen the pyramids. Where I worked as an educator, sixth-grade students studied Egypt as part of the social studies curriculum. If he were in one of our sixth-grade classrooms, that grandson would have had a very different perception from the kid sitting next to him because of his knowledge filter. It doesn't mean he was more intelligent or more motivated. But his perceptions were impacted by having been to Egypt, visited the pyramids, and ridden on a camel.

Teachers sometimes wish their students perceived things differently. For example, some students seem unfazed by their substandard academic performance, apparently oblivious to the long-term consequences. When students incorporate new information, their perceptions change. Students will consider new information – even painful information - if you have a positive relationship. This brings us to the third filter, the valuing filter.

Valuing Filter

We are evaluative creatures. We must evaluate to survive and thrive. Even those who claim to be nonjudgmental evaluate every bit of information they encounter. We ascribe a positive, negative, or neutral value to all incoming information using the following standard: Is this information need-satisfying?

The valuing filter is not simply a theoretical abstract, but supported by scientific study. Researcher Pierce Howard (1994, 150) writes: "When we receive 'news' from our environment, it is neither good nor bad until our appraisal process has passed judgment." What Howard calls the "appraisal process" is the valuing filter.

The evaluation of incoming information is automatic, wired into our genes, and tied to our need for survival. For that reason, it is literally impossible to be objective about incoming information. If we have negative feelings about someone, it significantly affects how we interpret information they offer. If you and I have a negative relationship and you try to help me see that my behavior is causing me problems, I will perceive you as meddlesome even if you are well meaning. On the other hand, if you and I have a positive relationship, I will perceive your comments differently. What you tell me may be difficult to hear but I will be more receptive to the information because I believe that you care about me and I value our relationship.

The valuing filter impacts how teachers perceive students and how students perceive teachers. To ensure that they are receptive to the information we want to share, students must see us as need-satisfying. When they value us positively, they might just profit from what we have to offer. The role of the valuing filter highlights the importance of developing positive relationships with students. Any educator who attempts to inspire quality without nurturing strong appropriate relationships with students is doomed to fail. (To be fair, there is an exception to this rule. If a student already has a strong relationship with the subject matter, they may do quality work even if they don't have a particularly close connection with the teacher. Those students are not the norm, however, as any teacher will tell you.)

A word of caution: Students sometimes engage in inappropriate behaviors because they are need-satisfying. For example, a student may put disrupting class into his quality world because it gives him power and freedom. I have had kids tell me they enjoy disrupting class "because it's fun." This is not a new phenomenon. In *I*

Wish, Stevie Wonder sang, "Smoking cigarettes and writing something nasty on the wall. Teacher sends you to the principal's office down the hall. You grow up and learn that kind of thing ain't right. But when you were doing it, it sure felt out of sight" (1976). How do we handle poor behavior? I find it helpful to remember the following principles:

- *Behavior is purposeful.* The purpose of behavior is to satisfy our basic needs. The basic needs are general, but behavior is always specific, so while there is a genetic instruction to have fun (general), there is no genetic instruction to disrupt (specific). A skilled teacher will try to figure out what need or needs the inappropriate behavior satisfies. If the student tells me that disrupting is "fun," my job is to help him learn to satisfy the natural desire for fun in a responsible way. When I help a student meet his needs, we are collaborating. I'm not trying to control him.

- *All of us are doing the best we can.* This does not mean that we operate at our optimum capacity at every moment. It means that all behavior represents our best attempt at a specific point in time to get what we want - even if we might think of something preferable several days, minutes, or seconds later. As an educator, my role is to assist kids in building capacity so "the best they can" becomes increasingly responsible, both academically and socially.

- *People have the capacity to do good.* The idea that students have the capacity to do good is especially helpful when dealing with troublesome behavior. It helps us focus on our mission: helping students learn to responsibly satisfy the needs built into their genes. Many students seem intent on disrupting the educational process. Some even behave violently. To manage these students successfully, remember that they *can* behave responsibly. The goal of an inspiring teacher is to help students satisfy their needs without turning to antisocial behavior. To put it bluntly, if you think a poorly behaving student doesn't have the ability to make better choices, the game is over and you are doomed. Inspiring teachers don't view the world through rose-colored glasses, but they don't give up on kids. Rather than saying a student can't do something, they say they can't do it *yet.*

It is easy for teachers to focus exclusively on academic issues and forget that we are working with fragile, developing children. When we fail to create an accepting, nurturing school environment, students can become disconnected, disinterested, and prone to violent acting out. We are all too familiar with stories of violence occurring in schools, places that should remain a safe haven for everyone. Many schools are becoming more intentional about engaging at risk students so they feel connected to the school community. Teachers generally know which students are most at risk for behaving violently. To minimize the chance of violence erupting in your school, engage and include all students. The "Connections" program described in *Activating the Desire to Learn* (Sullo 2007, 143) offers a simple, cost-effective way to ensure that every student in your school has a positive interaction with a teacher every day.

Those who worry that taking time to build a positive school climate robs teachers of precious academic time may find it useful to learn there is considerable research linking a sense of community in schools with student achievement. In one study, Eric Schaps states: "A growing body of research confirms the benefits of building a sense of community in school. Students in schools with a strong sense of community are more likely to be academically motivated" (2003, 31).

Summary

People are active – not reactive. We are internally motivated. We are born with universal drives, basic needs built into our genetic structure. Our experiences lead us to develop highly individualized quality world pictures, the source of all internal motivation. We will work hard for the things in our quality world because we believe they are need-satisfying.

Our three filtering systems – the sensory filter, the knowledge filter, and the valuing filter – impact how we construct meaning from the information we receive. The inspiring teacher influences all three filtering systems by making sure students are paying attention (sensory filter), providing students with information (knowledge filter), and showing respect for the students (valuing filter). As a result, more students put learning and working hard into their quality world.

Finally, the inspiring teacher creates classrooms where students can meet their needs by doing what the teacher asks. In such an environment, behavior problems are less frequent and more easily handled. There is improved academic performance and students value learning.

The more you know about choice theory and the psychology of internal motivation, the more you can inspire students to do quality work in your classroom.

Reflect, Personalize, & Implement

Reflect

- Do you believe people are internally or externally motivated?
- If people are controlled by rewards and punishments, is it fair to hold them accountable for their actions?
- What are some essential differences between our basic needs and the quality world?

Personalize

- Think of times when you have done high quality work. Were you internally motivated?
- Are you more driven by some needs than others?
- In what ways is teaching in your quality world?

Implement

- What will you do to help students put working hard and learning as much as possible into their quality world?
- Identify three specific things you will do to implement what you have learned in this chapter

CHAPTER 2

Brain-Based Learning

The best teaching is compatible with how the brain works. You don't have to be a neuroscientist or brain specialist, but having a better understanding of how we learn most easily and efficiently is indispensable. In Chapter 1, you learned about choice theory, internal control, and motivation. Internal control psychology and brain-based learning are mutually supportive. Familiarity with both will enhance your performance in the classroom and enable you to become an inspiring teacher.

This chapter reviews some major principles of brain-based learning. Because new research and applications are being generated so rapidly, I encourage readers to become familiar with current literature about learning and the brain. To learn more about brain-based learning, do a web search and consult the bibliography.

Brain Information For the Nonspecialist

The average brain weighs about three pounds and is composed of roughly 100 billion cells (Jensen 1996, 7). In comparison, a monkey has about 10 billion brain cells, but here's the important part: it's not the number of brain cells that matters. It's the number of connections these cells make. Since a typical neuron (an impulse-conducting cell) can make more than ten thousand connections, there may be in excess of ten trillion connections (synapses) in the brain (Russell 1979, 33). And it is the density of the brain, as measured by the number of synapses, which distinguishes greater from lesser mental capacity (Howard 1994, 38).

The ability of the human brain far outstrips the most sophisticated computer. The storage capacity of our brains is vast. Consider this: we can record a thousand new bits of information every second from birth to death before taxing our capacity. Furthermore, our brain is a multiprocessor. At any given time, it is processing color, movement, emotion, shape, intensity, sound, taste, and weight while identifying patterns and making meaning of incoming information (Jensen 1996, 8).

The slow, linear style of instruction used in many classrooms fails to maximize learning because the brain lacks enough stimulation. Most students thrive in an environment with significantly more input. Because a rich, multifaceted environment is more brain compatible, students are more engaged and discipline problems are dramatically reduced. Of course, there's a flip side to every coin. As much as students need ample input, they also need time to process and reflect for learning to last.

Left and Right Hemispheres

The brain is divided into two hemispheres. A band of fibers known as the corpus callosum runs between the two hemispheres and is the primary channel of interhemispheric communication. If the two hemispheres were not connected, information sent to the right hemisphere would be unavailable to the left hemisphere and visa versa.

Even though both hemispheres are involved in virtually every complex behavior, each hemisphere has primary responsibility for particular functions. Hemispheric specialization results in increased efficiency. The left hemisphere is more analytical and sequential. It is more linear in its reasoning and concrete in its orientation. In most people, the left hemisphere is more active when we are processing language. The right hemisphere is the more visual hemisphere. It identifies relationships instead of bits of information in relative isolation. The right hemisphere is more active when we are processing spatial relationships.

That said, hemispheric preference is not an absolute. As Russell reminds us, "When obliged to, either hemisphere can function in either mode" (1979, 53). Music, for example, is generally associated with the right hemisphere. Researchers have found, however, that professional musicians process music in the left hemisphere as well, making this activity more of a whole-brain enterprise.

Because there are so many exceptions to the common left-right tendency, it is best not to assume a particular activity is associated with the left hemisphere or right hemisphere for every learner. Instead, intentionally structure a learning environment that engages both hemispheres and maximizes the learning of all students. Inspiring teachers include activities that appeal to both the typical left-hemisphere orientation (sequencing tasks, literary activities, factual information, and a linear structure) as well as to the right-hemisphere (visual learning, open-ended questions, experiential learning, and moving from general to specific).

With 100 billion cells, the communication network within the human brain is both vast and complex. Information must pass from cell to cell, moving from the cell body of a neuron, an impulse-conducting cell, through the neuron's axon. At the end of the axon is the synapse, a small gap that separates two neurons. On the other side of the synapse is the dendrite, the receptor site of the adjacent neuron. The information then moves down another axon to the next synapse. Sufficient electrochemical energy is required for the neuron to fire, transmitting information across the synaptic gap. Neurons operate on an "all or none" principle:

either there is adequate electrochemical energy for the information to jump the synapse and arrive at the next neuron intact, or there is insufficient energy and the transmission stops. The number of synapses that must be successfully negotiated in even the most routine behavior is astounding.

Neurotransmitters (stored within the neurons and released when there is sufficient energy) are critical in the process of communication. The neurotransmitters move into the synaptic gap, carrying the information from the axon of one neuron to the dendrite of the next. Once the transmission is complete, the neurotransmitters are reabsorbed by the original neuron.

More than 50 neurotransmitters have been identified. Some of the most commonly known are dopamine, glutamate, endorphin, norepinephrine, and serotonin. Our level of neurotransmitters can significantly affect our perceptions, emotions, learning, and memory. Proper nutrition and exercise help us maintain appropriate levels of neurotransmitters. Inspiring teachers, regardless of what they teach and the grade level of their students, understand the importance of proper nutrition and exercise in building a more efficient brain.

Creating The Brain-Compatible Learning Environment

The inspiring teacher intentionally creates an environment where learning takes place most easily. Learning can be either conscious or nonconscious. Even though we spend hours developing learning plans for our students, most of what they learn is acquired nonconsciously. Jensen (1996, 44) explains, "When we say [conscious learning], we mean that we are aware of what we are learning, while we are learning it. Nonconscious learning means acquisition – we are taking it in, but there is no attention or awareness of it. Most classroom learning happens without the knowledge of the teacher." Dr. Emile Donchin says, "More than 99% of all learning is non-conscious. Your students are learning without knowing it. They are constantly picking up learning from visual cues, sounds, experiences, aromas and other environmental cues that far exceed any content from a lesson plan or course" (Jensen 1995, 35). In practical terms, that means we would be wise to consider much more than simply the learning plan we create for kids. It's important to consider all the extraneous factors that significantly impact what is learned.

Visuals

Inspiring teachers use posters and other peripherals to enhance the learning environment and take advantage of nonconscious learning. Visuals are especially effective because we take in more information visually than through any other sense. Literally millions of signals are processed every second in the visual centers of the brain (Wolfe 2001). In fact, the eyes contain 70 percent of our sensory receptors (Sylwester 1995, 61).

Since the attention of students will wane periodically no matter how engaging your lesson may be, ensure that wandering eyes encounter information that supports your academic objectives. Choose posters and other peripherals for their educational value, not merely to create an attractive classroom appearance (Tate 2004). Posters with inspirational quotations or tranquil scenes promote a relaxing environment that promotes learning. Major concepts and content can be displayed so that learners nonconsciously see them even when they don't seem to be paying attention. Exemplary student work can also be displayed in the room. To maintain a learning environment that is fresh and inviting, change visuals regularly.

Music

Numerous studies confirm the positive relationship between certain music and learning:

- A report delivered at the 1987 National Music Educators Conference indicated that students taking music courses in high school scored 20-40 points higher on standardized college entrance exams.

- A study conducted by a college entrance exam board found that students who studied music for four or more years scored higher in both verbal and math tests.

- Countries with the top science and math scores all have strong music and arts programs (Jensen 1995, 218).

- Steven Halpern writes, "Important new evidence shows that not only is the study of music beneficial in itself, but the introduction of [it] into a school's curriculum causes marked improvement in math, reading, and the sciences" (quoted in Jensen 1995, 219).

Music is not a frill, something to be cut when budgets need to be trimmed. Music and the arts contribute significantly to traditional academic learning. We cut them at our peril.

Researchers have discovered that listening to particular compositions by Mozart during instructional time can measurably enhance spatial learning, memory, and reasoning. In studies involving preschool, secondary school, and college students, computer-generated graphs of brain-wave activity look remarkably similar to Mozart's scores (Jensen 1995, 217). With more studies confirming the benefits of music in the classroom, it has become increasingly common to hear music playing.

Not all music has a positive impact on learning, however. Teachers should be judicious when playing music. If your goal is simply to play music, then anything will do and any time is fine. But if your goal is to enhance learning, then timing and selection are important considerations. As Jensen states: "Listening to Mozart before testing is valuable; listening during a test would cause neural competition by interfering with the neural firing pattern" (1998, 37-38).

I once heard a teacher tell her students, "If I can hear you over the music, you are being too loud." In this classroom, music was being used as a behavior management tool, but did little else to support academic excellence. Don't be so naïve to think student achievement will increase simply because you have music playing in your classroom. The issue is more complex.

When students hear something familiar, many will attend more to the music and less to the material you are presenting. For that reason, it is probably best to play music that students do not know. I have been in classrooms where students have been tapping their pencils and "lost in the music," oblivious to the science lesson being taught. Make sure that the music you use facilitates learning and does not unwittingly interfere with what you are trying to teach. Music should complement your teaching and remain in the background. When it moves into the foreground and competes with your instruction, music is counterproductive – unless, of course, you are a music teacher!

Using music more than 30 percent of the time is generally not a good idea (Jensen 1995, 221). Because of its calming effect, baroque music is especially effective when you want your students to relax and focus, perhaps at the beginning of class or when transitioning to a new activity (Lozanov 1991). Baroque music also promotes memory and has been correlated with higher test scores (Rose 1986). Finally, baroque music has been shown to be helpful when conducting a review as it helps students remember the concepts that have been introduced (Tate 2004, 61).

Music does not need to be used exclusively as subliminal background during instructional times. I have seen students create a rap to help them remember key concepts in a science class. Rhythm functions as a mnemonic device, allowing students to recall facts more easily. I have been in classrooms where teachers played high-energy music and had kids parade around the room until the music stopped. Once it stopped, they were asked to find a partner and ask a question about the content that had just been presented. In this case, the music was used to get students moving, find new learning partners, and review recently learned material. In my staff development workshops, I frequently use music and have participants complete an activity before a song is finished. This increases movement, energy, involvement, and helps participants complete tasks in a timely way. As you can see, there are numerous ways for inspiring teachers to use music to enhance learning.

Novelty and Ritual

We attend to anything unusual in the environment because novelty might mean danger. Building novelty into the learning environment increases student attention. Each time you introduce a new concept, you create a novel situation. Novelty alerts the brain to attend more closely, maximizing immediate learning. Introducing new material in a unique way makes it easier to develop stronger memories. (I will say more about memory later in this chapter.)

While there is value in novelty, there is also stress. Ritual and predictability offer relief from stress and are beneficial to the brain. The inspiring teacher structures a classroom that has many rituals so students know what to expect at certain times. An inspiring teacher may find it helpful to have calm, soothing, brain-compatible music playing when the students enter the room. Another ritual many teachers use is a "problem of the day" for the students to work on as soon as they arrive. A brief journal-writing time at the beginning of each class is a common ritual. The use of a daily ritual creates the feeling of security that characterizes any predictable environment. As you can see from these examples, classroom rituals don't necessarily have to be fun. From a brain-based perspective, the value of ritual is predictability, satisfying the need for safety and security, enabling kids to more comfortably handle the stress involved in learning something new.

Novelty and ritual are two sides of the same coin. The more ritual you incorporate, the more your learners can tolerate and profit from novelty. Too much novelty without sufficient ritual creates a stressful environment that inhibits learning. With adequate ritual and predictability in the environment, however, the brain thrives with increased novelty. A balance of novelty and ritual enhances academic achievement.

Providing Challenge and Feedback

The most productive learning environment is characterized by high challenge and low to moderate stress (Jensen 1995, 55). An insufficiently challenging lesson robs students of the opportunity to grow. Remember that we are genetically instructed to seek competence. In an environment with no real challenge, students have insufficient opportunity to satisfy the need for competence by engaging in rigorous academic work. In a challenging classroom, students who successfully master complex tasks satisfy the need for power in a productive, socially positive way. Inspiring teachers challenge students and support them as they struggle and grow.

In addition to challenge, students thrive when teachers provide ample feedback. As Jensen says, "Feedback makes for better brains and learners" (1995, 284). It's important to distinguish between feedback and criticism. Feedback is non-evaluative, providing information so learners can more effectively self-evaluate and improve the quality of their performance. Criticism is evaluative and hampers the natural drive to self-evaluate and improve. When criticized, students typically defend their actions instead of focusing on how to improve.

When a student submits a piece of writing, it can always be improved. Without specific quality feedback, however, there is little reason to believe that he can substantially improve his work independently. It is not enough to tell the student, "Keep working on this and return it to me when it's better." The student needs direction and specific feedback that he does not perceive as criticism.

The difference between useful feedback and well-meaning but unhelpful "constructive criticism" stems from how information is communicated. You want students to profit from what you say. If I were working with students on a piece of writing, I might begin by asking, "Do you want people to pay attention to your ideas?" Because of the universal drive for power and competence, the students will likely say yes. I would then say, "One of the things we work on in this class is how to write so people will listen to us and our ideas." Instead of telling the students that writing is something they "have to do," I want them to see writing as something they "get to do" and that better writing leads to increased personal power. Once this happens, we have a shared vision, an essential component of an inspiring classroom.

Next, I would tell the students that I am a more competent writer than they are. My feedback will be more helpful if they see me as an "expert." With that in mind, I might say, "I'm glad you want to become better writers because I can help you. I've been writing for a long time and I've had more practice than you. But first, I have a question. When you write something and give it to me, would it help if I told you what I especially liked and what areas need work?" Again, my goal is to develop a shared quality world picture so students perceive my comments as helpful feedback, not counterproductive "constructive criticism." By linking my feedback to their desire to improve their writing, they will perceive my comments positively.

Finally, I might ask, "Would it be easier to locate my comments if I used a color that stands out from what you use? If you write in blue or black ink, would my comments stand out if I used red ink?" Suddenly, students see papers peppered with editorial comments in red ink in a positive way. "Red" has been transformed from a negative to a positive because of how the information was communicated. This perception helps students use the editorial commentary as helpful feedback, not demoralizing criticism. What occurs might seem magical, but it's what happens when inspiring teachers communicate effectively.

Feedback helps the brain maximize its potential. Unless you are vigilant, it can deteriorate into criticism and interfere with learning and the natural quest for competence. Non-threatening, quality feedback accelerates the learning process and fosters a desire to become more academically skilled.

Emotion

Behavior has four components: acting, thinking, feeling, and physiology. The feeling, or emotional, component in learning is as important as the thinking, or cognitive, component. We remember events that are laced with emotion (Jensen 1998, 79). The stronger the emotion, the stronger the memory pathway that is created in the brain. Therefore, anyone who strips education of emotion inhibits learning.

The classrooms most conducive to academic achievement are those characterized by positive emotion. Remember from our discussion of the valuing filter in Chapter 1 that all incoming information is automatically assigned an emotional value. When students are in a positive emotional state during instructional time, they are more likely to remember what they have learned. Concluding an instructional activity with a celebration that has everyone in a positive frame of mind also makes the learning more memorable.

Expressing emotions minimizes the chances of them being bottled up. Suppressed emotions are apt to spill out in inappropriate ways, leading to unnecessary discipline problems (Jensen 1998, 79). By engaging positive emotions and infusing an emotional element into what we teach, we increase achievement and decrease disciplinary problems while structuring classrooms compatible with how we learn most easily and effectively.

Since experiences with a strong emotional content are more easily recalled, many of the following are present in an inspiring classroom: enthusiasm, drama, role plays, lively debates, hands-on learning experiences, guest experts, and laughter.

The Impact of Threat

Just as positive emotion enhances learning, negative emotion significantly reduces learning. Sadly, "For many students, school is a dangerous place. And when perceived as such, a learner's instinct to survive overrides the motivation for academic success" (Jensen 2011, 56). Any behavior that makes students feel threatened should be avoided.

When threatened, we shift into a survival mode. Our energy is spent ensuring that we survive the perceived threat. Blood, oxygen, and life-sustaining nutrients are sent to the large muscles, readying us for the well-known fight or flight behaviors designed to protect us. The result is decreased blood flow to the brain. The frontal lobes of the brain are the first affected and the area most compromised during times of stress and threat. The frontal lobes are involved in long-term planning, higher-level thinking, and problem solving. A student who feels threatened is likely to exercise less effective judgment, behave impulsively, and be unable to access effective problem-solving strategies. We want our students driven by the need to develop competence, not the need to survive.

Research conducted by Alan Rozanski (1988, 1005-12) suggests that sarcasm, criticism, and put-downs increase abnormalities in our heart rate. Here's the real scary part: these abnormalities were as significant and measurable as those from a heavy workout or pre-attack myocardial chest pains. There is no place in the inspiring classroom for either physical or emotional threat.

Lots of teachers use threat in the classroom. Why? The goal of threatening students is to get them to produce higher quality work and learn more effectively. There's nothing wrong with the intent, but what does the research tell us about the results?

There is no evidence that threats help students meet long-term academic expectations. In fact, "excess stress and threat in the school environment may be single greatest contributor to impaired academic learning" (Jensen 1998, 52). Teachers regularly lament the fact that too many students have difficulty identifying salient information. Gazzaniga has found that the stress brought on by threats impairs a student's ability to distinguish between what's most relevant and what is less important. The stress and threats frequently used in too many classrooms exacerbates the problem. Sylwester finds the problem so disturbing that he writes: "School environments that cause continual stress reduce the school's ability to carry out its principal mission" (1995, 38).

Despite the underlying positive intent, threats undermine achievement, encourage disruption, devalue learning, and create an atmosphere that makes school unpleasant for teachers and students alike.

Positive Learning States

Brain researchers define a state as "a distinct body mind moment composed of a specific chemical balance in the body" (Jensen 1996, 49). There are numerous states, some better for learning than others. The inspiring teacher both reads and manages states effectively to enhance learning.

Each state has its own package of behaviors. In a challenging, low-stress environment that provides ample feedback, students are more likely to be in states that optimize learning. The specific state you desire will differ depending on what you want students to do, but the following are all compatible with learning: curiosity, anticipation, suspense, challenge, and temporary confusion. The inspiring teacher elicits these desirable states, preparing the students to be fully engaged in the lesson. For instance, as students enter the room, they may see a question on the board that captures their interest and has them curious before class has even begun. As long as students believe they can overcome challenges by working hard, then temporary confusion is helpful. Confusion causes disequilibrium and confident students quickly take action to regain feelings of balance and competence.

Learn to read students' states. When you scan the classroom and sense the students are growing bored and disengaged, you need a state change. Instead of plowing ahead so you can say you "covered the material," acknowledge the counterproductive state and help students move into a state more conducive to learning. For example, your class may be zoning out because they have been maintaining attention for an extended period or they are experiencing the all-too-familiar "after lunch slump." Before you lose them (and invite the behavior problems that accompany disengaged, unproductive students), have the students stand up, find a learning partner, and review what you taught in the last ten minutes. Each student might be required to ask a partner two specific questions and discuss how they can apply what they have learned. As students stand up, move, interact, and process what you have taught, the state of boredom will be replaced by a state of engagement, curiosity, or other states that will support your academic objectives.

Brain-based theorists often say that all behavior is "state dependent." The behavior you observe reflects the state of your students. When you are curious, you use your "curious behaviors." When you are angry, you use your "angry behaviors." When you are bored, you use your "bored behaviors." If you want student behavior to change, change the state.

Students behaving inappropriately are in a specific state. As long as they remain in that state, they are limited to the behaviors associated with it – most of which are not welcome in school. The most effective way to deal with unwanted behavior in school is to help students change states. Once they move out of the less desirable state and into one more appropriate for school success, their behavior will change dramatically, almost instantaneously. Engaged, curious students don't access their "annoyed," "bored," "angry," and "disconnected" behaviors.

One desirable learning state is "flow," which occurs when a task is neither too challenging nor too easy. Csikszentmihalyi (1990) writes, "Challenges that are greater than your skills, that's anxiety. When your skills exceed the challenges, that's boredom." When you have the skills to successfully meet a challenge, you enter a state of flow. All effective teachers seek to create an environment where learners are in a state of flow. Based on continuous, informal assessment, they offer students a chance to stretch themselves, be temporarily confused, persevere, and develop new skills. While there is no recipe to create flow, you are most likely to succeed when you provide an exciting environment that uses cooperative learning teams, challenges learners to do their best, and minimizes stress, pressure, and unnecessary deadlines.

Paying Attention and Making Meaning

Teachers frequently say they want students to pay attention so they can learn, but there is a profound difference between paying attention and deep learning. While paying outward attention is necessary to gain new information, it is equally important for students to turn their focus inward to make meaning for themselves. Learning only occurs when externally accessed content has been internally processed. "Meaning is always generated from within, not externally" (Jensen 1998, 46).

For learners to access new information, they must be externally focused and pay attention. Once information has been taken in, it is essential that students focus internally to make meaning of the content they have received. Each of us must sort out information in our own head, an internal process.

It is impossible to simultaneously pay attention (external orientation) and make deep meaning (internal orientation). Students who are too attentive fail to make adequate meaning; they learn material in a rote, superficial way. Consider students who focus exclusively, often laboriously, on the process of decoding. They are so externally focused that their comprehension of the material they have read is abysmal. Or the student who is hyper-focused on a spot on the ceiling – "Hey, is that a bug? It looks like it's moving." – rather than reflecting on the material just presented in class. They are certainly paying attention. They just aren't making meaning.

Conversely, those busy making meaning when teachers want them to pay attention are at a disadvantage because they are doing so without adequate input. Because they fail to pay adequate attention, they make meaning with limited information. As a result, the meaning they create may be inaccurate.

Remember: All we get by paying *external* attention is access to information. Making meaning from that information is an *internal* process.

Inspiring teachers introduce new material with energy and emotion, engaging students' attention. They help kids appreciate the relevance of what they are studying and connect it to prior learning.

To assist students' internal meaning making, give them a few minutes to process what they have learned. For example, after introducing a new concept, you may ask them to take out their journals and summarize what has been introduced. You may ask them to stand and discuss the new learning with a partner. You may ask them to draw a picture that reflects what they learned. These simple strategies (each involving different learning modalities) will help your students make meaning of the information you have just introduced and help them place it in long-term memory. It can't be overstated: if you want kids to retain what you taught and learn at a deep level, give them adequate process time to make meaning.

Nutrition

A healthy diet supports optimum academic achievement. While it is the responsibility of parents to provide students a healthy diet, educators play an important role by providing nutritional information to students. It is remarkable how little students know about proper nutrition and a healthy diet. Students are often painfully ignorant about the impact of what they eat. Because most serious health problems related to poor diet do not manifest until later in life, it is appropriate for us to educate our students now in this area.

Teachers can also model healthy nutrition. Research continually informs us that students learn much more from what we show them than what we tell them. When they see teachers eating a healthy snack and a healthy lunch, they will learn more from that than they learn in any number of presentations about positive eating habits.

Schools can also provide informational newsletters to parents. Of special interest to many parents would be recipes that provide for proper nutrition on a limited budget. Too many parents fill their kids with empty calories because they are unaware that healthy alternatives can be prepared in a cost effective way.

Foods that promote a healthy brain include leafy green vegetables, salmon, nuts, lean meat, and fresh fruit (Connors 1989). Studies suggest that vitamin and mineral supplements may also support leaning and memory (Ostrander and Schroeder 1991). At a brain-based learning workshop held in June 1996, Eric Jensen offered the following nutritional ideas:

- Eggs, fish, turkey, tofu, pork, chicken, and yogurt can boost alertness and mental performance.

- Egg yolks and wheat germ can enhance memory.

- Folic acid, found in leafy green vegetables, beef liver, and beans, can reduce depression and boost learning performance.

- The trace mineral boron, found in broccoli, apples, pears, peaches, grapes, and nuts, improves mental activity.

- Brain specialists recommend drinking 8 to 12 glasses of water a day. (By encouraging students to drink water, even in class, you can make a difference in their lives. Students who lack adequate amounts of water often display symptoms commonly associated with attention deficit disorder or behavioral disorders.)

- Foods rich in iron, such as dark-green vegetables, meat, and fish, can enhance attention, memory, and visual-motor coordination.

- Polyunsaturated fats, unlike saturated fats, lead to increased learning and memory.

Other Factors Affecting The Learning Environment

Color in the classroom impacts learning. According to researchers, the most calming color is sky blue (Jensen 1995, 57). While this color may seem like an attractive option, remember that you don't want your students too calm. In general, dark colors lower stress and increase feelings of serenity. Bright colors, such as red, orange, and yellow, are riskier. While they can excite and energize, they also can increase aggressive and nervous behaviors. (*Note*: If you have lots of kids eating in the school cafeteria, you might want to stay away from brightly painted walls unless you're trying to discover just how much energy a bunch of kids can generate in a less structured environment with minimal adult supervision!)

Research suggests that the best colors to enhance learning are yellow, beige, and off-white. It is important to emphasize that these comments are generalities and that your individual personality and state at any given moment influence how a color affects you. For example, if you are already highly stressed, red may lead to aggression. On the other hand, if you are relaxed, red may be appropriately engaging and inviting.

Many classrooms are equipped with fluorescent lighting. Research has suggested that this light source can contribute to restlessness, fidgeting, and other symptoms associated with ADHD (Jensen 1995, 60). Ideally, classrooms would take advantage of natural light and supplement this with full spectrum lighting and lamps. In addition to more attentive behaviors, students in classrooms with natural and full spectrum lighting have been found to have better attendance (Jensen 1998, 54).

Research conducted at Rensselaer Polytechnic Institute in New York found that students developed more ambitious goals, took on greater challenges, and got along better with peers when exposed to certain aromas (Jensen 1995, 65). The aromas that appear to facilitate alertness include peppermint, basil, lemon, cinnamon, and rosemary. Lavender, chamomile, orange, and rose are helpful in calming and relaxing. (*Note:* Be sure to consider potential allergies and sensitivities before considering introducing certain aromas into the classroom environment.)

Plants enhance the learning environment because they remove pollutants and replenish oxygen. Research studies conducted by the Federal Clean Air Council found that plants not only raised oxygen levels but also helped increase workers' productivity by 10 percent (Jensen 1995, 64).

There are numerous ways the environment can be structured to facilitate increased productivity and enhance learning. While there are factors that affect learning over which we have little or no control, we can take simple steps that maximize learning for every student in the classroom.

Memory

It was once believed that memories are akin to literal recordings of real-life events. We now know that memory is a creative, reconstructive process. Daniel Schacter, professor at Harvard Medical School, said at a presentation in Boston on June 20, 1997, "We are the intervening issue between the world and what we create in our memory." Memories are not encoded as a whole and neatly stored in one part of the brain. Instead, bits of information are stored in various parts of the brain. "Remembering" involves constructing a representation of reality from fragments in a way that necessitates creativity and subjectivity.

To recall an experience, we need cues provided by association. The more associations we create when we encounter new material, the easier it is to recall that material when we need it (Russell

1979, 100). This complex process is facilitated by the tendency of the brain to create multiple associations when presented with novel information. Remember, the brain pays more attention to things that are new. "The more distinctive and memorable you make the learning situation, the better will be your memory of the material studied" (Russell 1979, 107).

Things are more easily recalled when a person is in the same state and location as when the original learning took place. If you want your students to effectively access previously learned material when testing them, recreate the original learning state. For example, if students listened to a particular sonata by Mozart while studying the American Revolution, have the same music playing during your assessment. The music provides a nonconscious association, facilitating access to what was learned. Because we store memory by location, it is easier to remember things when we are "back at the scene." For that reason, testing where the learning occurred will yield the best results. If you provide direct instruction in the science lab and test in a different classroom, your students will not recall the information as easily as if you teach and test in the same location.

The more unique a learning experience is, the more easily the brain creates associations to remember the material for later use. Those uncomfortable with gimmicks or tricks intended to enhance memory should remember that the brain naturally creates associations. Peter Russell (1979, 129) says, "It is not that mnemonics are cheating, but rather by not consciously using them, one is effectively hindering the learning process. The brain is, in the end, going to form associative connections whether you help it or not." To facilitate learning and memory, provide your students with mnemonic devices when you instruct. Mnemonics are consistent with the natural tendency of the brain to look for patterns and associations (Chapman 1993). Mnemonics also engage both semantic and automatic memory pathways and the more pathways utilized, the greater chance of recalling information (Sprenger 1999).

We hold information in our short-term memory for about five to twenty seconds. For information to be moved into long-term memory, we need to create an association. Help students create associations through such things as mnemonics, emotion, storytelling, metaphor, and appropriate focus during instructional time. Inefficiently stored (unassociated) information may be "known" but unavailable. The more we create uniqueness with new learning, the more easily information can be retrieved. Encoding information without sufficient distinction is like giving all your word processing documents the same name. You know the information is somewhere on the hard drive, but it will be a slow, laborious process to locate it when you need it.

Inspiring teachers regularly assess if learners can transfer learning to different contexts and different states. Ultimately, learning must be "portable:" students need to bring it with them wherever they go and not just access what they know when they are in the same location and in the same state as when the learning occurred. For the best results, introduce material so students create as many effective associations as possible. First assess their knowledge in situations that mimic the original learning. Gradually, have them demonstrate that they "own" the learning by showing you they can recall the information in different locations and under different conditions. When students have reached that level, they have truly mastered the material.

Types of Memory

While we often speak of memory in general terms, there are different types of memory. *Semantic memory* is our memory for speech and text and is the least reliable memory system. When we ask students to remember facts from books or presentations, we are tapping into semantic memory. Competent students without strong semantic memories may not do particularly well on tasks like this. Ironically, traditional classroom evaluations primarily rely on the least reliable memory, semantic memory. To minimize the negative impact of evaluations that highlight semantic memory, be certain your students create strong multiple associations at the time new learning takes place.

Episodic memory is memory embedded within a given context, typically a location or experience. For example, you are in the kitchen and think, "I need the notebook in my bedroom for tonight's class." When you get to the bedroom, you can't remember why you're there! You know you went there on a specific mission, but you can't remember what. In these circumstances, many of us retrace our steps. Once back in the kitchen, where the thought originated, we suddenly remember, "Ah, yes. The notebook."

To strengthen your students' episodic memory, routinely ask them to visualize the context in which learning took place. As students become skilled in this strategy designed to access episodic memory, they will discover that they are able to remember much more than they thought possible. We can easily improve our memories when we practice visualizing the conditions where learning took place. Have students practice mentally returning to the scene of the learning and visualizing the episode with as much detail as possible. As they create these memories, associations will help them remember significantly more than they thought they ever knew.

Memory from hands-on learning experiences is called *procedural memory* and is among the strongest of memories. Many adults who have not ridden a bicycle for years still ride with relative ease because the requisite skills have been stored in the body.

While we may not remember what we have heard or seen as easily (semantic memory), we are much more likely to remember what we do (procedural memory). To strengthen memory, get students physically engaged and moving as they learn. Have them create and not just recite. There are many reasons why it is wise to increase movement in the classroom. Simply standing up increases oxygen and blood flow to the brain and increases alertness (Jensen 1995). When we are physically active, we create memories in multiple locations in the brain, increasing the probability of us remembering the material at a later date (Rizzolatti et al. 1997). And over two decades of replicated research affirms that movement creates an appropriate state for learning (Thayer 1996). Students who perform, who participate in a vigorous debate, or who create a product will be much more likely to access those memories because the associations have been wired into their bodies.

Finally, considerable repetition or learning with a particularly strong emotional component creates *reflexive memories*. For many of us, multiplication facts are remembered effortlessly because of the repetitive nature of drills. Frequently used phone numbers are similarly stored in our reflexive memory. (At least that was true before smart phones eliminated the need to remember most phone numbers.)

We also reflexively remember events that include a strong emotional component. Most people who were at least ten years old have vivid memories of what they were doing and where they were on November 22, 1963, when they heard that President Kennedy had been shot. The same is true for September 11, a day of unspeakable horror that will never be forgotten.

Each memory pathway – semantic, episodic, procedural, and reflexive – is separate. Even when we store information using multiple memory systems, our ability to recall is limited to the specific pathways we can access. When we evaluate student learning and only activate semantic memory, we will only discover a fraction of what the students have learned. The inspiring teacher does everything possible to activate as many memory pathways as possible so that students demonstrate exactly what they know.

With the emphasis on high-stakes testing, it is more important than ever for teachers to ensure that students create strong, accessible memories and that we provide evaluations that accurately measure what our students know. When we equip students with strategies that enhance their memory, we will find that test scores improve and more schools are able to achieve the Adequate Yearly Progress required by No Child Left Behind. In short, we don't just need to teach better; we need our students to demonstrate what they have learned. Currently, too many students fail to show what they know, an unfortunate reality that can be addressed with relative ease.

Gardner's Theory Of Multiple Intelligences

Until recently, students were often identified as "intelligent" or "less intelligent." While we remain guilty of using this immensely broad descriptor, there has been a revolution concerning the nature of intelligence. No one has contributed more than Harvard professor Howard Gardner to our understanding of the nature of intelligence. In his landmark 1983 publication *Frames of Mind: The Theory of Multiple Intelligences*, Gardner suggests there are numerous ways to conceptualize intelligence. It's not as simple as a student being "smart" or "not so smart." Today Gardner suspects that there are even more than the seven discreet, identifiable domains he originally identified.

Gardner believes that people with ability that is highly valued in a given culture are seen as more intelligent than those who have skills and abilities in less-valued areas. He argues, therefore, that our perception of intelligence may be little more than a reflection of cultural bias and values. Since what is valued in one culture may not be valued in another, intelligence is not as fixed or objective as we imagine.

The seven intelligences originally proposed by Gardner are:

- **Logical-mathematical:** This sequential thinker is generally strong in mathematics and problem solving.

- **Spatial:** This thinker has a keen ability to manipulate forms and objects in space.

- **Interpersonal:** This thinker has strong people skills and is good at conflict resolution, listening, and persuasion.

- **Bodily-kinesthetic:** This thinker tends to have good motor skills and values physical and athletic ability.

- **Verbal-linguistic:** This thinker enjoys talking, reading, and most activities involving language.

- **Intrapersonal:** This thinker enjoys being alone and is especially skilled at goal setting and self-evaluation.

- **Musical-rhythmic:** This thinker is particularly sensitive to the nuances of sound (timbre, pitch, rhythm).

More recently, Gardner (1999) has added an eighth intelligence:

- **Naturalist:** This thinker is especially skilled at recognizing, categorizing, and drawing upon certain features of the environment.

Other areas Gardner continues to explore include both spiritual and existential intelligence. To date, he has not garnered sufficient evidence to identify them as discreet areas of intelligence.

Each person has relative strengths and weaknesses in these separate domains. The intelligences are completely independent, so ability in one area doesn't predict ability in another. Gardner's theory of multiple intelligences gives us a new way to think about our students. As Jensen (1995, 182) notes, *"How smart are you?* is now irrelevant. A more powerful new question is, *How are you smart?"*

Schools generally continue to emphasize two intelligences: verbal-linguistic and logical-mathematical. Students skilled in these areas have the best chance to be successful in school, a clear advantage later in life. If Gardner's notion of multiple, separate, independent intelligences is valid, then we can help more students experience school success by creating learning environments that appeal to as many intelligences as possible.

With complete respect and appreciation for Gardner's theory, I offer this word of caution to teachers. Part of our job is to equip students with skills to succeed in society. Help kids cultivate each of the intelligences, but remember that verbal-linguistic and logical-mathematical intelligence are still the most valued in many cultures. We do students an unintentional disservice if we don't prepare them to succeed in areas that matter most in their society.

The Brain-Based Curriculum

In days past, teachers frequently had significant control over the curriculum, if not on an individual level, at least on a departmental or district level. When I began my career as an English teacher, I was given broad latitude about what to teach. Guidelines were provided to me so I would prepare my students for the rigors of the tenth grade English curriculum, but the specifics were left to my discretion. Even when learning outcomes were articulated, I had complete freedom to decide what to teach so the students achieved the objectives.

Times certainly have changed. Today, most curricular decisions are made on the state or national level. While most teachers retain considerable autonomy about how to teach, they have far less say about what to teach.

Even though teachers have had to sacrifice some autonomy, I believe that some uniformity of content has improved education. In a mobile society, there is wisdom in providing common curricular experiences to students from different areas. It minimizes the gaps in learning that plague many students who move frequently. It ensures that there is more equality in the educational experience offered to students regardless of where they are born or where they might move. In a society where there is competition for desirable employment, providing equal educational opportunities is essential.

Brain-based learning is more concerned with the "how" of teaching than the "what." Even though curricular decisions are typically made at a district or state level, teachers can offer virtually any content to students in a brain-compatible way. That's what the inspiring teacher does. Students are taught to appreciate the value of learning and doing their best work.

Relevance

The most compelling curriculum is one that students perceive as relevant. Since the brain is designed to help us survive, it will attend most closely to what it identifies as essential. If input is not relevant, it is less likely that neurons will transmit it and create lasting memories (Jensen 1998). You may perceive the curriculum to be meaningful and relevant, but don't assume the students know that! It's imperative that you communicate to students *why* your lesson is important, meaningful, and relevant. Inspiring teachers help kids appreciate that what they are being asked to learn is valuable and deserves their attention and effort.

One way to increase the relevance of what you teach is to link it to what students already know (Marzano 1992). This creates additional connections, improves memory, and makes the new learning more accessible. When appropriate, have students work on projects. Research suggests that when we work on authentic tasks, we create stronger neural connections and the material becomes more meaningful and relevant to learners (Westwater and Wolfe 2000).

When students perceive what they are learning as relevant, they are more likely to be actively engaged, improving achievement. The student who asks, "Why do we have to do this?" or "Why are we studying this?" is giving you a chance to explain the relevance of your lesson. Don't see it as a sign of disrespect or a behavioral infraction. Take it for what it is: a natural search for meaning. The classrooms I observe where students work the hardest and learn the most are those where the teacher ensures that the students perceive the lesson as useful and relevant.

Interdisciplinary Experiences

Because the brain is a multiprocessor, we learn best when immersed in an interdisciplinary experience. The brain does not process information in a lock-step, sequential way. In the real world, we take in massive amounts of information and make meaning by creating complex webs and connections that blur arbitrary lines of subject matter. Learning is not neatly compartmentalized into subject areas. School learning, particularly in secondary schools, is typically separated into rigid subject categories. A brain-compatible school offers considerable interdisciplinary work and opportunities for thematic learning.

Teachers in a self-contained classroom, common in elementary schools, can easily create interdisciplinary lessons. Since many middle schools are organized in teaching teams, teachers can collaborate on interdisciplinary units of instruction and assignments. When I taught English, each spring the science teacher on my team taught a unit that required field research and the completion of a research paper with a traditional bibliography. At the same time, I taught the students how to write a research paper. Because the students saw the two instructional units as connected, they put more effort into their work and learned more than if we taught these skills in isolation. As a middle school administrator, I supervised teachers who taught both English and social studies. The most effective ones taught writing and reading skills in context, using the social studies curriculum.

Admittedly, developing interdisciplinary units in a traditional high school is considerably more difficult. It takes effort, administrative leadership, and might even involves deviating from the traditional matrix schedule. Thankfully, more and more high schools are developing small, flexible learning communities that support interdisciplinary instruction. It may be convenient for adults to divide the day into subject specific periods, but this structure doesn't maximize learning. If we are serious about improving our schools, and we really mean it when we say we act with the best interest of students in mind, we would be wise to revamp how we structure our schools and courses of study.

Focus on Skills

The brain-compatible learning environment focuses on underlying skills more than specific content. We want students to read well and to become lifelong readers; we are less concerned about which books students read. However, today's more rigid curriculum means that much of the content is mandated, so we owe it to students to emphasize essential content. At the same time, inspiring teachers are always fundamentally concerned with helping students master fundamental skills and processes. When there is little flexibility in the curriculum, explain to students why they are being asked to do specific tasks so they do not see them as arbitrary.

In-Depth Study

Ordinary teachers focus on what they *cover*. Better teachers focus on what they *teach*. In the best classrooms, the emphasis is on what the students *learn*. Whenever possible, inspiring teachers offer students the opportunity to study selected topics in depth. This practice results in less material being covered, but the material taught is learned well.

Taking into account the developmental level and ability of your students, give them projects that allow them to immerse themselves in learning a great deal about an interesting subject. If you use interdisciplinary instruction, students will be even more engaged in relevant work that addresses curricular requirements in multiple areas when working on a single project. Once students are mature enough, encourage them to engage in independent study and projects, especially those that involve reading, research, and writing. When they complete a project, they can share their findings with classmates, perhaps inspiring others to deepen their learning as well. When students demonstrate expertise in an area, they satisfy their need for competence. When they teach their peers, they deepen their learning.

Assessment & Evaluation

Used interchangeably by many, assessment and evaluation are not the same. Assessment identifies where students are. It is descriptive, not evaluative. Evaluation is a judgment about how students are performing, often with reference to where they "should" be.

Assessment

Ongoing formative assessment is part of good teaching. Teachers continually assess what students know and are able to do so they can provide learning opportunities that stretch kids without overwhelming them.

In the most effective classrooms I visit, teachers assess student progress routinely. They often ask students to assess their own performance: "If you understood the last problem, give me a thumbs up. If you are not sure you get it, give me a thumbs sideways. If you are still confused, give me a thumbs down." Instantaneously, the teacher has valuable feedback and knows if the class is ready to move on or of some kids need additional direct instruction.

Ongoing assessment is vital. Teachers need to know where their learners are so they can select the next activity. Literally dozens of times each class, teachers make decisions about what to do next. Inspiring teachers are not held hostage by a pre-determined lesson plan. Rather, they continually assess what students know and can do so they provide instruction that matches the readiness of their students.

Assessment is more art than science. It is impossible to tell exactly what students know, have learned, and can do. Still, imprecise assessment is superior to none at all. Inspiring teachers regularly gather the most reliable data they can to identify where learners are and what should be taught next.

Evaluation

Evaluation is overtly judgmental. Whereas assessment says, "This is where you are," evaluation suggests, "This is where you are and this is where we expect you to be."

One of the most onerous evaluative practices we engage in is comparing one student to another. Ranking students has little to do with learning. Our traditional system of assigning letter grades is an evaluative practice that represents one of the least enlightened and most brain-antagonistic notions ever created. As I noted in *Inspiring Quality in Your School* (Sullo 1997, 182), I would forego letter grades and instead provide detailed information to students and parents about what appears to have been learned according to the evidence available to the teacher.

While my comments about traditional evaluation and grading seem radical to some, they are supported by brain research. Eric Jensen writes, "Many educators think they measure learning every day. They don't. Neuroscientist Gary Lynch of the University of California at Irvine says learning is defined by synaptic growth, connections among dendrites and changes in the density of neural networks. Do you have a test that measures that? Biologist Ira Black ... says that learning is defined by 'modifications to the neuronal pattern of connectivity.' Do you have a test that measures that?" (1996, 118). Jensen also notes, "Biologically, the best, most valuable and deepest learning does not produce any tangible results for a considerable time" (1995, 277).

For the foreseeable future, I expect we will continue to evaluate students against each other, although I wish we would simply emphasize feedback so learners could self-evaluate and improve the quality of their work.

For those who believe that we need to compare students, the only relevant data is how the performance of a student compares to what that same student demonstrated previously. That is information that students, teachers, and parents can use.

Inspiring teachers use evaluation to enhance learning. Ask students to apply what they have learned. Have them articulate how the learning has changed them. Have them create a tangible product that shows what has been mastered. A well-constructed bookcase crafted by a student who previously did not have the skills to build one, for example, is tangible evidence that learning has taken place. A letter to a local politician that gets an answer shows that a student can express ideas in writing with a degree of competence. A well-written research-based report is evidence that a student knows how to gather, analyze, evaluate, and present information.

The real world provides feedback that lets us know whether we have been successful. We should do nothing less in our schools. Inspiring teachers identify the indicators of quality. When criteria are clearly articulated, and teachers instruct students in how to master the required skills, evaluation can enhance learning.

Summary

Inspiring teachers create learning plans and academic experiences that are compatible with how we learn most easily and efficiently. Internal control psychology provides a theoretical foundation from which to operate. Brain-based learning is a research-driven model about how we learn. Together with an understanding of the important developmental issues addressed in the next chapter, they provide the base on which inspiring teachers build their classrooms. Using a sound theory of human behavior and the most current information about how the brain works, and creating an environment sensitive to the developmental needs of learners gives every teacher a chance to become inspirational in the lives of students.

Reflect, Personalize, & Implement

Reflect
- Identify some important features of a brain-compatible classroom.
- What is the impact of fear and threat on learning?
- What "states" are most conducive to learning and which are least conducive?

Personalize
- Do you think students should pay attention all the time?
- Do you agree with Howard Gardner that there are different intelligences?
- What do you do to ensure that your instruction and assessment is brain-compatible?

Implement

- What will you do to ensure that your classroom is a "brain compatible environment"?
- What will you do to help your students enhance their memory?
- What will you do to help your students remain in an optimal state for learning?

CHAPTER 3

Developmental Issues

Stephen Covey (1989) recounts an experience he had while riding the subway in New York. A man and his children entered the quiet subway car where Covey was sitting. The children began running up and down the car with little parental supervision. Believing that the father was shirking his parental responsibilities, Covey chided him only to discover that the family had just left the hospital after learning that the children's mother had died. With this information, Covey developed a radically different perception of the grieving father and the traumatized children.

How often do we think we know "the" truth? Just like Covey, we can all make erroneous judgments when we don't have complete information.

Teachers encounter a wide range of behaviors every day. With classrooms becoming increasingly heterogeneous, the following fact is especially relevant: typical students in a classroom – those not identified with significant developmental challenges or handicaps – can vary developmentally by as much as three years (Jensen 1995, 12). Teachers need a solid understanding of developmental issues and the typical and atypical behaviors expressed at certain ages.

Buck's Theory of Development

Nancy Buck (1997) has proposed a developmental model based on choice theory, the internal control psychology discussed in Chapter 1. She suggests that we are born with genetic instructions - the basic needs: connecting/belonging, power, freedom, fun, and survival - but without the behaviors to meet those needs. Because we begin our lives dependent on our parents or other primary caregivers, a cooperative relationship ensures that we will be provided for during our period of dependence. At the same time, we need to compete to survive independently and our need for autonomy drives us to develop skills to transition from dependence to independence. This dynamic sets up the primary developmental imperative of childhood: learning to be cooperative enough to be taken care of while being competitive enough to survive independently.

Buck identifies connecting and fun as cooperative needs because we usually use cooperative behaviors to satisfy them. Power and freedom, on the other hand, are competitive needs because we frequently use competitive behaviors to satisfy them. Throughout childhood we are sometimes driven more by cooperation and sometimes driven more by competition. While Buck offers "typical" age ranges for each developmental cycle, they are only general guidelines. More important is the alternating movement between the drives to cooperate and compete.

The primary need during the first eight months of life is survival. From about 8 months to 16 months, infants and toddlers focus more on cooperative behaviors that support the drive to survive. Infants, for example, learn to coo, smile, make eye contact, and play peek-a-boo, all engaging, cooperative behaviors that maximize their chances of being well cared for during this period of dependence.

Between about 16 and 20 months, most toddlers enter the "terrible twos," a period when competitive behaviors dominate. During this stage, which typically lasts about six months, toddlers yearn for freedom. With only a rudimentary vocabulary, they resort to screaming, throwing a tantrum, or hurling objects to get their way. At this point, kids learn that sometimes they get what they want by being competitive as well as by being cooperative. While parents frequently complain about this phase, it is an important developmental period because children need to develop competitive behaviors to succeed in life. Those who only meet their needs using cooperative behaviors are seriously limited as adults.

Throughout early childhood – approximately every six months – children move from a more cooperative phase dominated by the needs for belonging and fun, to a more competitive phase dominated by the needs for power and freedom. Along the way, children expand their repertoire of cooperative and competitive behaviors.

Neither cooperation nor competition is wholly satisfying. Cooperating inhibits our desire to take risks and explore the world. Competing separates us from others. This dynamic tension perpetuates the cycle. Even though children strive to satisfy both the cooperative and the competitive needs, one type is more dominant during a given phase and less dominant during another. Buck suggests that even when they are in a competitive phase, children frequently abandon competitive behaviors and revert to cooperative behaviors if they feel their safety is threatened.

This has important classroom implications. In fear-laden classrooms, children may behave more cooperatively at the expense of the exploring, reaching-out, and risk-taking behaviors associated with increased academic achievement. Inspiring teachers create classrooms that support children when they are in the competitive phase while also providing sufficient structure so this drive can be followed safely and respectfully.

The six-month cycles continue until children are about seven years old. Phases then lengthen to eight, nine, or ten months, giving children more time to develop effective and increasingly complex cooperative or competitive behaviors.

In adolescence, competitive behaviors are especially prevalent. Legitimate authority is often challenged, sometimes in inappropriate ways. Although inspiring teachers do not endorse poor behavior, they understand that the primary developmental tasks of adolescence are separation and the formation of an independent identity. Inspiring teachers understand the behavior of adolescents for what it is – an attempt to separate, to individuate, and to flourish during a developmental phase when competitive behaviors tend to dominate. Our job as adults is to help adolescents move through this critical phase as gracefully as possible. More than at any other time in their lives, adolescents need our understanding and support.

Even when competitive drives are particularly strong, adolescents still feel cooperative urges. They may separate from adults by adopting styles that are different from their parents, finding comfort by dressing just like their peers. At the same time, many adolescents also want the approval of parents and teachers. Not knowing how to communicate this desire without sacrificing the independence they so desperately crave, they may appear aloof and distant. Inspiring teachers help adolescents feel safe and connected as they move toward separation and independence, sometimes in awkward, challenging ways.

The competitive drive is especially strong in early adolescence. By the time most students reach age 16, cooperative behaviors begin to reemerge, and students use them almost as regularly as competitive behaviors. Teachers who work with students in middle school and the early high school years need to know how to deal with students in the competitive phase. These teachers need to create a task-oriented, academically focused learning environment, that supports students' drive toward competitive behaviors, autonomy, and separation.

Teachers working with students in the competitive phase are more vulnerable to being drawn into power struggles and arguments. When challenged, it's easy to resort to "power-over" behaviors, unintentionally modeling an irresponsible use of power when adolescents desperately need to learn how to compete fairly and effectively. Only teachers who have effectively met their own need for power are able to handle this situation well. Others get into arguments, even shouting matches with adolescents. While this might provide immediate satisfaction – reminding the adolescent who is the boss - it models inappropriate, bullying behavior and prevents adolescents from engaging in the crucial developmental task before them: learning how to compete fairly and respectfully.

The skills you need to be an inspiring teacher depend on the age of your students and their developmental level. Buck's model of human development suggests that teachers working with elementary school students and students nearing the end of high school will encounter both cooperative and competitive phases. Those working with students in middle school through the first two years of high school will encounter more competition than cooperation. To bring out the best in others, you need to understand what drives students, what needs dominate at any point, and how to structure a developmentally appropriate learning environment that maximizes achievement.

Stages of Moral Development

With all due respect to No Child Left Behind, Adequate Yearly Progress, the Common Core Curriculum, and the importance of academic competence, we should never lose sight of the fact that we educate the whole child. A student's moral development is every bit as important as his academic development – even if there is never an exam that will quantify what we teach.

Lawrence Kohlberg's ideas about the development of moral reasoning are among the most important in psychology. Thomas Lickona (1983) builds on Kohlberg's contributions and teachers will find Lickona's work useful for two reasons.

- It provides a snapshot of typical student behaviors at various ages and stages.

- It suggests how to help children move to a higher level of moral reasoning.

Let me be clear: I am in no way proposing that we try to accelerate the normal developmental process. David Elkind (1981, 1984, 1987) has written eloquently and extensively about the dangers of hurrying children. At the same time, it is appropriate to provide students with learning opportunities when they are developmentally ready.

Like Buck and other developmental experts, Lickona stresses that age ranges he suggests are only general guidelines. Many healthy kids will enter or leave specific stages earlier or later than the norm.

A synopsis of Likona's stages of moral reasoning follows.

Stage One: Preschool and Kindergarten Years

The preschool and kindergarten stage generally emerges between the ages of four and a half and five. (*Note:* Other stages precede this one, but they are outside the scope of this book.)

Behavior at this stage is marked by obedience and cooperation. Children's moral reasoning is based on a belief that only one viewpoint, that of adults, is valid. Their compliant behavior stems from a simple premise: we obey so we will not be punished. At this stage, children tend to obey because they believe adults are all-knowing and any transgressions will be discovered. Children are likely to tattle frequently, believing that breaking the rules should result in punishment. They often violate rules when adults are not present and the threat of punishment is removed, however, because they have not internalized the rules. If you ask children at this stage why rules should be followed, they'll refer to the need to avoid punishment. This is true even for children who have experienced little punishment.

The moral reasoning of young children might suggest that they are amenable to an approach based on external control psychology. They follow rules to avoid punishment, an external orientation. You might think this proves we are externally motivated, but don't be fooled. There's a big difference between behavior and motivation. Children at this stage are just as internally motivated as anyone else. They are internally motivated by their quality world picture to be obedient, adult pleasing, and compliant.

According to Kohlberg, we can understand a moral orientation that is one level higher than the one at which we operate (Lickona 1983). Anything beyond that is of no value, since the reasoning is too complex to be understood, but the next level of reasoning is well within our grasp. Inspiring teachers, therefore, facilitate the transition to the next stage of moral reasoning.

The next stage of moral reasoning for preschool to kindergarten children emphasizes fairness. Teach children to empathize, to imagine what it is like to be on the receiving end of an unkind comment or a wayward fist. For children at this stage, keep concepts concrete. Instead of saying, "I would like everyone in this class to be treated fairly," ask "How would we behave in this class if we treated one another fairly?" This moves an abstract concept – *fairness* – into concrete actions that young students understand.

Always avoid comments that target the lowest levels of moral reasoning. The teacher who says, "I never want to catch anyone in this class acting that way!" is appealing to the lowest level of moral reasoning: you obey to avoid being punished. Comments like this unintentionally teach kids that what matters is not getting caught.

Finally, at this stage children do not yet understand "why." It's developmentally normal for them to have no clue why stealing is wrong. We can still, however, teach them that stealing is not sanctioned.

Stage Two: The Early Elementary Years

Most children have moved into stage two by the time they are seven or eight. Although older children develop more advanced reasoning in later stages, they'll revert to stage two tendencies with some regularity throughout childhood and adolescence. As Likona observes, "Stage Two is alive and well in most of us adults" (1983, 134).

In stage two, the rule-bound, compliant child of stage one has been replaced by a child driven by freedom, independence, and individuality. A host of challenging behaviors generally accompany the drive toward independence. To succeed with these children, keep in mind that they are limited by what they know how to do. When working with children in more challenging stages, remember that all behavior is purposeful and all of us, including young children, are doing the best we can. The inspiring teacher understands that children are attempting to establish independence and assists them in developing responsible behaviors to achieve their goals.

While stage one children are unable to appreciate more than one point of view, stage two children operate from the position that everyone has their own point of view. Children at this stage are demanding, egocentric, and believe it is acceptable for people to do what they want. They see themselves as equal to adults in many ways and begin to assert that they have rights. They are likely to resist anything they see as bossing them.

Fairness is a major concern for students in this stage. Because they operate concretely, stage two thinkers define fairness as everyone getting the same treatment. They are consummate dealmakers. "I'll be nice to you if you are nice to me" makes perfect sense to them. Being nice is not inherently valued. It is valued because relationships should be reciprocal. Of course, the reverse works equally well for stage two thinkers: "If you are mean to me, it is only fair that I am mean to you."

With increasingly heterogeneous classrooms, teachers must accommodate diverse needs while respecting the stage two demand for equality. The task is difficult, but inspiring teachers have been successfully undertaking it for years. While there is no one "right" way to meet this challenge, here are some ideas about how to proceed.

- Bear in mind that stage two thinkers perceive fairness as equality and that they highly value this concept. To engage the students and respect their developmental level, address the issue of fairness openly. Create a shared vision of fairness with your students by explaining that it's important to you as well. That simple declaration will help build positive relationships with your students.

- Help stage two thinkers develop an expanded notion of what fairness means. In his presentations, Rick Lavoie (*How Difficult Can This Be?* 1989) explains, "Fairness does not mean that everyone gets the same thing. Fairness means that everyone gets what he or she needs." Honest, respectful dialogue with young children helps them perceive fairness as more than simple equality and is an example of helping nudge kids along to a higher level of moral reasoning.

Some adults share the stage two belief that fairness means equal treatment. Teachers in this category sometimes struggle with heterogeneous classes – especially those that include kids who need significant modifications - and differentiated instruction. By expanding their definition of fairness to mean that we all get what we need, these teachers will inspire more students and probably derive more enjoyment from teaching.

Because stage two students are more assertive and less fearful of adults, they can engage in blatantly mean behavior. Such unsavory behavior is developmentally expected and fairly predictable. The preoccupation with equality leads to more conflicts, and young students frequently cling to their negative emotions until they get payback. When your students engage in inappropriate behavior, ask yourself, "What can I do to help these students successfully negotiate this developmental phase? What is the most helpful way to perceive them and their behavior? What can I say to them and do with them that will help them move forward in a socially appropriate and respectful way?" Focus less on imposing consequences – although there may be consequences – and assist students through the developmental process. One way to handle mean behavior is to appeal to the students' sense of fairness. Because fairness is paramount to stage two thinkers, an appeal to fairness will be heard.

If appealing to fairness fails, invite students to move forward by suggesting that kindness is an even more important value than fairness. They will only shift their thinking if two conditions are present. First, you need a strong, positive relationship with them. You are, after all, asking them to transcend a developmentally compelling value. Second, you need to model that you value kindness more than fairness. Teachers traditionally value fairness. If you ask your students to demonstrate allegiance to another value, they will automatically check whether you behave in a way that suggests kindness is more important than fairness. What they have seen from you will determine how seriously they consider your suggestion to move beyond a primitive "equality principle."

Stage Three: The Middle Elementary Years and Beyond

In many ways, stage three is the most interesting stage of moral reasoning because of its complexity. Some students move into this stage during the middle elementary years, but others don't reach it until much later. Stage three is characterized by trying to please others. Depending on when it emerges, stage three moral reasoning is either a welcome change or an incredible challenge.

If students move into stage three before adolescence, adults are usually ecstatic. There is a return to obedience and a desire to please. In school, these students are easily managed. If, however, kids move into stage three at the onset of adolescence, it's an entirely different story. The desire to please is just as strong, but the reference point becomes the peer group instead of adults. As a result, stage three adolescents are particularly susceptible to peer pressure.

Stage three thinkers care deeply about how others see them. They work diligently to gain approval. If that sounds like external motivation, remember that the desire to be thought of positively by others is in the quality worlds of stage three thinkers, so they are very much internally motivated.

An appealing quality of stage three thinkers is their ability to see things from another's point of view. In part because they are so preoccupied about what others think of them, they are particularly sensitive to how others feel. Having moved beyond a narrow understanding of fairness, they are often generous and compassionate. Stage three thinkers accept and even endorse a teacher having different expectations for different students.

To appeal to your students' desire to cooperate, ask questions such as the following: "Would you like to be known as honest, hard working, and responsible?" Instead of using power and imposing consequences, work with students at this stage to resolve problems collaboratively. Stage three thinkers especially appreciate this approach. They want to cooperate, and problem solving is a developmentally appropriate task for adolescents.

During adolescence, students naturally want more independence. Inspiring teachers don't struggle against what is developmentally written into our genes. At the same time, appropriate adult authority is essential for academic achievement. Allow freedom within a well-structured environment that students perceive as reasonable and worth supporting.

Stage Four: Adolescents and Adults

Stage four thinkers shift from a focus on personal relationships to an emphasis on connection to a group. Whereas stage three thinkers seek approval and are likely to succumb to peer pressure to maintain personal relationships, stage four students are concerned about being good members of this class, this school, this gang, this clique, this larger society. The capacity to move beyond individual relationships means these students can enter into a social contract. Stage four thinking is at the heart of a democratic government. It is what allows us to put aside our personal desires for the good of the larger society. In this stage, students begin to move beyond independence toward interdependence.

Students at this stage appreciate that their actions affect others. At earlier stages of moral reasoning, students behave with less sensitivity in part because they are unaware of the ramifications of their actions. Stage four students feel compassion for people with whom they have no personal relationship, provided they are part of the same system.

Stage four thinkers value the need to cooperate, although they can behave in uncooperative ways. Inspiring teachers appeal to stage four thinkers' belief in the importance of cooperation for the good of the system. Those students who achieve stage four understand what is involved in being a functioning member of a larger system. Teachers can ask students to consider "what we do in this school" and "how we want to be seen." Provided they are connected to and invested in the school, stage four thinkers will adopt behaviors that help the school function smoothly.

Some of the most successful social institutions and businesses thrive because of stage four thinking. The United States is built upon stage four moral reasoning. The Constitution serves as the belief system against which we measure and evaluate our actions. While we are a nation of individuals, we believe that no person is above the law or the principles set forth in our Constitution. Many schools and businesses craft mission statements to serve as their constitution against which all actions are evaluated.

Many students never move beyond a stage three orientation. Given the right environment, however, adolescents can move toward stage four. Some even demonstrate signs of this kind of moral reasoning in middle school. While teachers have no control over the homes in which students live, we can create schools that promote the moral reasoning skills of students.

Teachers inspire their students toward stage four moral reasoning in many ways. They help students realize that we are increasingly interdependent. As students acquire information about the world, they become more sensitive, knowledgeable, and appreciative of those around them. Inspiring teachers also facilitate discussions about social and moral issues, encouraging students to think about the relationship between the individual and any larger system (class, school, team, community). Such discussions naturally lead to considering what it means to be a responsible person. Inspiring teachers avoid telling students what they "should" do, letting students discover that for themselves.

Stage five, the highest level of moral reasoning, is characterized by respect for the rights of each individual and the belief that none of us should abdicate our moral responsibility. Because so few people operate from this perspective regularly and because individuals rarely attain this stage until they are in their twenties or beyond, it is not addressed here.

The development of moral reasoning, a critically important area, is often overlooked in education. But school is much more than an academic experience. Inspiring teachers prepare students to be positive contributors to our society and our world. Teaching academics is essential, but it is not enough. Regardless of the mandates that surround us, part of our mission is to prepare students to take their place as citizens in a democratic society. Understanding the stages of moral reasoning and developing strategies that encourage a student's growth are indispensable tools for inspiring teachers.

Stages of Cognitive Development

Much of what we know about cognitive development derives from the pioneering work of Swiss psychologist Jean Piaget. (Biehler 1981). Although many others have built upon the foundation he provided, Piaget remains a giant in the field of cognition. Piaget's greatest contribution can be expressed simply: children think differently from adults. Previously, children were generally thought to have less knowledge than adults but to process information in the same way.

Piaget's contributions are congruent with the internal control psychology belief that we actively construct meaning from our experiences using existing knowledge. Because young children have a different set of experiences from adults, they process information differently and construct very different meaning from identical input.

The fact that children process and create so differently from adults underscores the limitations of spoken language. While we may speak the same language as children, we communicate and understand differently. Communication through spoken language is a high-risk endeavor under the best circumstances. Communication through spoken language between child and adult has tremendous potential for misinterpretation. When errors in communication occur, inspiring teachers appreciate that they are as much to blame as the child is.

Piaget developed a four-stage model of cognitive development. Like other theorists, he stresses that the age ranges he uses are merely guidelines. The sequence of cognitive development, however, is predictable. It is also important to note that children drift between stages, moving ahead or regressing from time to time.

Piaget's first stage, the *sensorimotor stage*, occurs during the first two years of life. The first stage of importance to teachers is the *preoperational stage*, typical of children from about two to seven years old. The primary cognitive task during this stage is the mastery of symbols, which explains why language develops rapidly during this particular period. Children in this stage tend to center their attention on only one variable when solving problems. For example, children who are shown that two containers of different heights hold equal amounts of water still insist that the taller container holds more because they focus exclusively on the height of the containers, excluding other variables.

Sometime around the age of seven, students move into the *concrete operational stage*. For most kids, this stage lasts until early adolescence. To maximize their learning, students at this stage need to physically manipulate objects or to have had direct, concrete experience with them. Given the chance to manipulate materials, students at this stage can mentally reverse actions, something they were unable to do at the preoperational stage. They will still be confounded by hypothetical situations and will struggle with abstractions. Students may do well with geometry, a highly visual subject, provided they have opportunities to create tangible models. These same highly motivated and academically capable students might, however, struggle with algebra unless the teacher can transform this abstract subject into something concrete.

Beginning about age 12, many students show behaviors characteristic of *formal operational thinking*, the most complex thinking Piaget postulated. Formal operational thought is characterized by an ability to generalize, to engage in abstract thinking, and to develop and test hypotheses mentally. During middle school and even high school, students move back and forth between concrete operational and formal operational thinking. Their erratic performance and behavior can be frustrating, but inspiring teachers understand that is the nature of human development. That is why you should make learning a hands-on, tangible experience regardless of what you teach and the age of your students. Even formal operational thinkers will frequently downshift to concrete operational thinking and profit from learning activities that involve manipulation of physical objects. Help students think abstractly while accepting that many continue to need a more concrete orientation.

Inspiring teachers offer challenges and opportunities to students in different cognitive stages. They understand that *how* instruction is delivered is as important as the intellectual potential of the students. Intelligent students who are given instruction that does not match their cognitive stage will not learn as much as those who are less gifted but who have been given appropriate instruction.

Stages of Psychosocial Development

Psychologist Erik Erikson developed an eight-stage model of psychosocial development (Biehler 1981). While familiarity with all stages is recommended, only the two stages that relate to school-age children are discussed here.

Industry vs. Inferiority

Children between the ages of approximately 6 to 11 fall into the stage Erikson calls *industry vs. inferiority*. During this stage, the need for power or competence is a primary concern. Schools are especially important during this phase because the classroom is one arena where the need for power can be satisfied in a responsible, growth-enhancing way. Students who work hard and experience success in elementary school are better equipped to meet the challenges offered in secondary school. But this goes beyond kids getting good grades. It involves the creation of a strong work ethic. Inspiring teachers create classrooms that encourage students to demonstrate competence, master skills, and develop a sense of industry that will serve them the rest of their lives.

In nearly forty years in education, I have not encountered that many students who *couldn't* do high quality work, but I have seen far too many who *wouldn't*. Teachers, counselors, administrators, parents, and students all agree that most kids are capable of achieving academic success. What most struggling students lack is the work ethic or sense of industry required to succeed.

Everyone wants students to develop a strong work ethic. Unfortunately, most teachers cling to the "carrot and stick" model of external control psychology and reward young students for academic accomplishment. Stickers, awards, "Student of the Month," and other rewards are the norm in elementary schools everywhere. "What's wrong with that?" you ask? As EJ Sobo says, "Children cultivated toward dependence on external praise through constant positive stroking are at risk for growing into poorly-adjusted adults who must always look to others for approval. They never have a chance to develop their own internal resources" (2012).

Rather than giving students an external reward for achieving, inspiring teachers ask students how they feel after doing quality work that required considerable effort. As students reflect and self-evaluate, they discover that hard work and accomplishment feels good. By regularly providing opportunities for students to self-evaluate and affirm that hard work leads to a state of satisfaction and well being, you will help them develop the work ethic lacking in most underachieving students.

Identity vs. Role Confusion

From about 12 to 18 years old, students are in the stage termed *identity vs. role confusion*. Our identity makes us unique and recognizable despite all the physical changes that inevitably occur over time. If we don't establish a stable identity, we go through life like a rudderless ship, lacking a sense of who we are and continually reinventing ourselves. The central task of adolescence is beginning to form this stable identity.

One of the first signs that students are entering this phase is the adoption of crude "trial" identities. Whereas younger students identify with their parents and embrace many adult values, adolescents want to differentiate themselves from adults in general and their parents in particular. Adolescents sometimes take on identities that are the opposite of their parents', often devaluing everything their parents value. What is frequently perceived as defiant rebelliousness is simply the beginning of the process of separation that culminates in the formation of an independent identity. Because early adolescents don't have a lot of life experience, they often begin the process of identity formation by taking an oppositional stance: "I may not be sure exactly what or who I want to be, but I know that I don't want to be like my parents. So anything that reminds me of my parents – from clothes to music to political and religious ideas – I will reject and I will embrace the opposite."

In situations where children have been particularly close to their parents and have blindly accepted parental values, the separation process can be especially difficult and result in the formation of what Erikson called a "negative identity," a temporary identity that is opposite from the previous one. Because of the developmental imperative to create an identity, even a negative one is preferable to having none at all. Erikson cautions adults not to judge adolescents too quickly or too harshly as they go through this phase. To use his language, if we "confirm" the temporary identity by labeling a student a "delinquent," we increase the chances of the student permanently adopting that identity. It is crucial to separate the student from the behavior.

Let me give an example. Suppose an adolescent is caught with drugs. While there may be unpleasant consequences and we should not ignore the problem, it is best not to label the student a "drug user." Some will find this suggestion disturbing. "If a student uses drugs, isn't he a drug user?" they will ask. Of course, but there is little value in the label. In fact, there is potential for harm whenever we label adolescent behavior. The label offers the adolescent a way to avoid the primary developmental task of adolescence. Instead of doing the difficult work of building a true identity, they can adopt a prepackaged "druggie" identity with little effort. Since having an identity – any identity – is so compelling, the adolescent only needs to continue his drug use and his developmental struggle is over. He no longer has to confront the difficult questions that characterize adolescence: "Who am I? What is important to me? What are my true values?" Identified as a druggie, the struggle to "become" dissipates.

Adolescents can engage in outrageous behavior, some of it potentially deadly. This needs to be addressed, but never confirm a negative identity. Adolescents are in the process of becoming. What they ultimately become will be influenced by how we treat them as they move through this stage. As they test drive new roles and accompanying behaviors, it is crucial to remember that they are literally "works in progress." We want students to grow into adults who are caring, responsible decision-makers. Pierce Howard suggests, "Be reasonably accepting of selfishness and impulsivity among youth, knowing that – with understanding parents and societal nudging – the tendency is for people in their twenties to move toward a more cooperative and goal-focused adulthood" (1994, 141).

It is unlikely that students will have completely formed their identities by the time they leave high school. For most of us, the process continues well into our twenties even under the best of circumstances. Still, with appropriate support, many adolescents begin building a strong foundation for a unique identity during their high school years.

Summary

Assisting kids as they move through the developmental process is one of the most important things we do as educators. The focus today may be on test scores, but we do much more than prepare students academically. We have a responsibility to the whole child and need to consider developmental issues from numerous perspectives. Among other things, development includes psychological, moral reasoning, cognitive, and psychosocial issues. Without adequate understanding of typical developmental, we can easily misinterpret the behavior of students and treat them in ways that are counterproductive and fraught with unnecessary stress and tension. While each child is unique and no one fits any model perfectly, familiarity with the information in this chapter will help you be more effective.

Reflect, Personalize, & Implement

Reflect
- Do you agree with Buck that students cycle through cooperative and competitive phases?
- Identify the moral, cognitive, and psychosocial stages of the students you currently teach.

Personalize

- Why is it important for you to have a grasp of developmental issues?
- How can a knowledge of developmental issues enhance your teaching?

Implement

- What specific steps will you take to align your teaching with the developmental level of your students?
- How will you structure your class to facilitate your students' transition to the next developmental level without "hurrying" them?

PART II

APPLICATION

CHAPTER 4

The Qualities of an Inspiring Teacher

Since individuality and personal style are essential attributes of every inspiring teacher, there is no formula. What works beautifully for me might be a disaster for you because it doesn't reflect who you are. And I can't just do what you do and expect it will be successful, especially if it's forced or artificial. While there is potential value in observing a master teacher in action, I encourage you to heed the words of Ralph Waldo Emerson who reminded the graduating class of Harvard in 1838: "The imitator dooms himself to hopeless mediocrity." The inspiring teacher is far from mediocre. Having said that, most gifted teachers share certain attributes. In this chapter we will examine some of these traits. As you read, think about what qualities you already possess and how you can cultivate others to maximize your effectiveness.

Develop Positive Relationships

Inspiration is nurtured in relationship, so the single most indispensable quality in becoming an inspiring teacher is to cultivate positive relationships with your students. If you know your subject matter but don't connect with your students, you will only be successful with highly motivated students. Other students may do enough to get by, but you will never inspire them. You know those kids who skate by with a "C," seemingly satisfied even though you know they have the capacity to do much better work? Inspiring teachers understand that a positive relationship with these students is essential if you want them to be more successful. They are as committed to building strong relationships as they are to developing exemplary units of instruction.

Think about teachers who have inspired you. Almost certainly they demonstrated that they valued you, respected you, and were there to help you. They expected you to do your best, but it wasn't the detached, top-down "expectations" that characterize much of the standards movement. It was heart-felt and you never doubted that they had your best interests in mind as they taught you. It wasn't about making sure the school made AYP. It wasn't about ensuring that the teacher received a positive evaluation. Those things are natural by-products of a positive relationship, but their expectations were based on the fact that they cared about you, your potential, and your future. That kind of relationship has the capacity to inspire and is the kind of relationship that every student deserves.

Creating positive relationships is not always easy. Students can behave inappropriately, either consciously or unintentionally. They won't always appreciate the value of what you are trying to teach and they may do less than their best work. They'll sometimes act disinterested or bored, or may even be overtly hostile and defiant.

It makes perfect sense to disengage from students when they display negative behavior. If you do, however, you'll forfeit your opportunity to inspire disconnected students and unleash their positive potential. Without your support, these students will continue to underachieve, disrupt the learning of others, and make it difficult for you to enjoy your job. To inspire these students, you must first develop positive relationships with them. Connect with them and help them see the value of academic engagement and achievement.

I worked with a high school staff some years ago over a two year period. When we started discussing the importance of positive relationships, one of the teachers said something like this: "Most of our students are nice kids and it's easy to have positive connections with about 95% of them. But to be blunt, about 5% of the kids are jerks." I answered that it was our professional responsibility to develop connections with *all* students, not just the ones who "deserve" it. To be as blunt as this teacher, let me suggest that there's nothing special about building a positive relationship with "nice kids" who generally work hard and do what we ask them to do. What distinguishes the inspiring teacher is their commitment to connect with every student, whether they have "earned" it or not.

Begin by treating *all* students with respect and dignity – even when they behave in unacceptable ways. I used to tell students I would respect them and be honest with them regardless of how they chose to act. I wouldn't show respect only when kids earned it. If I did that, I'd be giving my power and autonomy to them. I refuse to let my behavior be determined by how another chooses to act.

Of course, these comments are made after nearly forty years as a professional educator. I didn't start my career with a full appreciation of the importance of positive relationships. Early in my first year as a ninth-grade English teacher, I was giving a spelling test and Tammy was obviously copying from her neighbor's paper. I moved near her table – a strategy that has since been identified as "proximity" - but she didn't stop, so I quietly asked her to move. When she asked me why, I simply repeated my request.

Quite unexpectedly, Tammy stood up, kicked her chair over, yelled, "Well, *#*# you!" and stormed out of the room.

Back then, I was clueless about the importance of relationships. I was young and naïve, believing that as long as I was well prepared and organized, I would be a successful teacher. Tammy was suspended from school for her outburst. When she returned, common sense led me to interact with her as little as possible and common sense yielded a predictable result: we both got through the year, but I never inspired her. She could have learned so much more. I could have been so much more successful as a teacher. I don't blame myself because I didn't know any better, but today I would handle the situation differently. I would actively try to engage Tammy. I would make it clear that as offensive as her behavior had been, I was still there to help her be successful. I would not tolerate her inappropriate behavior, but neither would I allow her actions to keep me from reaching out to her. I would not be controlled by her anger. I would help her grow.

I was reasonably successful as a classroom teacher because I related positively with most of my students. Without compromising my authority, I made it clear to the students that I liked them. We laughed a lot. We enjoyed each other. We were partners in the quest to become more educated and more skilled. Although I had occasional problems, they were handled with relative ease because the students and I genuinely liked each other. When students and teachers have positive relationships, there is little motivation to be disruptive. Increased learning is a virtual certainty and inspiration a viable possibility.

Be Passionate About Learning

Inspiring teachers are passionate about learning. Many are synthesizers, pulling together seemingly disparate concepts and weaving them into a meaningful whole. Inspiring teachers recognize that new experiences enrich them, making them more valuable resources for their students.

A passion for learning may express itself in traditional academic learning, the earning of advanced degrees, and the development of specific curricular expertise, but a passion for learning is not restricted to educational and academic pursuits. It may manifest as an enthusiasm for travel (traveling to distant lands and experiencing other cultures helps the inspiring teacher make the classroom come alive!) or it may be seen in the development of particular hobbies. Those who are passionate about learning – regardless of the topic – help students appreciate that learning is fun and enriching in its own right.

Regardless of their skills and credentials, inspiring teachers never stop learning. They often put themselves in situations where they are unskilled, creating the opportunity to once again experience the challenge, fear, excitement, and fun of learning something new. An inspiring teacher I know immerses himself in new learning in his retirement years. It's a delight to listen as he talks with excitement, energy, and enthusiasm about his discoveries. He was a school psychologist in New York City for many years. Today he is the guy I first contact when I have any questions about any of my Apple products.

Another inspiring teacher (a master teacher and former state teacher association president) told me that she intentionally set out to have at least one new learning experience every year. The content of the new learning was largely unimportant. Her goals were to experience the feeling of incompetence that comes with any new learning, to learn to embrace that feeling rather than fear it, and to be open to new ways of thinking and being. She told me it helped her develop greater empathy with her students as she introduced concepts that were familiar and manageable to her but new and intimidating to them. Being familiar with the feelings associated with new learning strengthened her relationship with her students.

Show Enthusiasm For What You Teach

Movies are filled with humorous examples of monotone teachers clearly bored out of their minds putting their students to sleep. While this makes for enjoyable entertainment, it's no way to run a classroom. Excitement is contagious. Spread it! The most inspiring classrooms I visit are ones where the teacher is clearly excited about the subject. Even young students can tell when their teachers love what they're teaching and when they are simply going through the motions.

Most teachers appreciate the importance of their content. Show the kids that you enjoy what you do and help them develop a love of and appreciation for what you teach. If you look bored and disinterested, it sends a clear message to kids that doesn't inspire the hard work and commitment that supports deep learning. I'm sure you wouldn't teach it if it weren't worthwhile. Don't be afraid to share your enthusiasm for your subject and inspire your students to develop a desire to immerse themselves in rigorous, enriching academic work.

Match Words And Actions

While conducting a workshop some time ago in Lockport, New York, a poster in the room caught my attention: "If we don't model what we teach, we are teaching something else." Inspiring teachers model what they teach.

Congruence is respected and fraudulence is always unmasked. The tyrannical teacher who teaches the value of democratic principles never inspires. The writing teacher who is never seen with pen in hand or fingers on the keyboard will have difficulty convincing students that writing is a worthwhile pastime.

What bothers students more than anything else is when they perceive teachers to be hypocrites. They tolerate demanding teachers. They accept low grades when they believe they are being treated fairly. What they cannot abide is when they sense a discrepancy between what a teacher says and what is actually done.

You are always modeling - whether you want to or not. Students pay attention to your actions. Do your actions match what you preach? As long as your words and actions match, you have the capacity to inspire.

Love And Appreciate Children

A love of your subject matter is helpful but insufficient. In fact, if you care more about your subject than you care about students, you will never inspire. You will be successful with those who already value your subject, but that is good teaching, not inspiring teaching.

To be an inspiring teacher, it is essential that you love and appreciate kids. To inspire students who have no clue why it's worth learning what you are trying to teach, you must first demonstrate that you care for them.

Of course there will be times when you may not enjoy your students. To have those moments on occasion is normal. There's no such thing as a perfect relationship. But if you dislike large numbers of students and complain about students in general, you probably are in the wrong profession.

It's true that teachers today face more challenges than their predecessors did. But it's also true that students today can be inspired to produce quality work and to take pride in doing their best. When kids act like kids and you find yourself smiling, you're on the right track. Don't encourage disruptive behavior, but understand that students sometimes will be disruptive. Your love and appreciation of children, even when they behave inappropriately, never diminishes.

Maintain A "Both-And" Orientation

It is easy to get caught in the "either-or" trap. Either you support high standards and academic achievement, or you want students to enjoy school. Either you support the notion that education should be humanistic and nurturing, or you favor high stakes testing. The list goes on.

It's not that simple. Inspiring teachers reject the "either-or" trap and adopt a "both-and" orientation. They accept that high-stakes testing, No Child Left Behind, Adequate Yearly Progress, Common Core State Standards, and similar academic rigors are part of the current landscape. But they also know that to inspire the highest academic achievement in our students, they must create nurturing, supportive schools and classrooms. Inspiring teachers deftly merge disparate points of view to create challenging classrooms where students thrive academically and socially.

While many of their colleagues ignore the child and teach to the test, or abandon high expectations so they can create a nurturing classroom, inspiring teachers understand that these two views are not inherently incompatible. Don't be distracted by false dichotomies. The ASCD Whole Child initiative is one example of a "both-and" orientation, affirming "Each child, in each school, in each of our communities deserves to be healthy, safe, engaged, supported, and challenged." For more information, visit http://www.wholechildeducation.org/.

Control What You Can Control

Education is filled with things we can't control. The list is long and includes things such as state mandated testing, No Child Left Behind, Common Core State Standards, parent support, class size, and the cognitive ability of students. Many teachers spend considerable time and energy worrying and complaining about variables over which they have little of no control. The result is an overwhelming feeling of hopelessness that frequently leads to burnout or cynicism. Teachers preoccupied with issues they *can't* control have less energy available to address those issues they *can* control.

Inspiring teachers are pragmatic realists who have a clear understanding of what they control. They know that they impact their classroom and the relationship they create with their students, colleagues, and parents. They focus on creating lessons that are engaging and maximize student learning, regardless of how many students they have or the make-up of the class. They do not let their energy be depleted by focusing on extraneous matters. Rather, they focus on their students and their professional responsibilities.

It's not that other matters don't concern them. It is simply that inspiring teachers are efficient about their use of time and energy so they can create the most satisfying professional identify for themselves.

As Sylwester states: "What we have is a classroom full of students who come with genes and nonschool experiences. We're not responsible for the genes, and we usually can't directly do anything about the experiences that students bring to school – but we are responsible for the quality of their school experiences. It's our job to make sure that school experiences enhance the development of a student's brain" (1995, 139).

Be Professional

Inspiring teachers never forget that they are professionals. They know that developing a positive relationship with students does not mean they are "buddies" with the students. They are friendly without being friends. While they clearly communicate to their students that they care about them, they maintain appropriate boundaries and establish a respectful authority within the classroom.

Part of being professional means that inspiring teachers are in their assigned areas on time. They are prompt to class and other responsibilities, even ones they don't especially enjoy. They evaluate and return student work promptly, modeling for their students the professional behavior they value.

Other Qualities Of Inspiring Teachers

I often begin staff development workshops by asking the teachers to identify the qualities they hope I will display during our time together. Regardless of where I go, teachers consistently ask that I:

- Be open-minded.

- Facilitate a learning environment where they feel valued and believe they can make important contributions to the group.

- Provide concrete strategies and model what is to be accomplished.

- Communicate an enthusiasm for the subject matter.

- Help them understand that learning will be worth the effort.

- Display a sense of humor, making sure it is always respectful, not hurtful.

- Demonstrate a thorough knowledge of the subject matter.

- Be flexible and allow teachers to achieve learning objectives in various ways.

- Respect participants unconditionally.

Even if I do all of this, it doesn't guarantee success. It's not just what I do: it's also what I don't do. So once we have compiled a list of qualities teachers positively value, I ask them to identify what will interfere with their learning and success. Participants typically ask me not to do the following:

- Repeat ideas unnecessarily.

- Talk in a monotone and teach lethargically.

- Talk "at" or "down" to them.

- Belittle or berate them.

- Seek to gain approval from the group at the expense of an individual.

- Disengage.

- Ask participants to accept responsibility for their behavior while refusing to accept my responsibilities as the instructor.

- Ask participants to do something that I am not willing to do.

In most cases, the educators who attend my workshops are compliant and eager to learn. In other words, they're a joy to teach. Even so, I have to engage in certain behaviors and avoid others to inspire them and maximize their learning.

Now consider a typical classroom, someplace slightly less ideal. Not every student is compliant. Not every student is eager to learn what you want to teach. Not every student has a history of academic success. Under these conditions, it is even more crucial to embody the qualities that inspire achievement and steer clear of behaviors that compromise learning. All of us would be wise to take the advice given to me by my workshop participants.

Summary

All inspiring teachers are unique. Despite their many differences, however, most inspiring teachers share certain qualities.

- More than anything else, they develop positive relationships with their students. They communicate why working hard to achieve is important and they help students grow academically and socially.

- Inspiring teachers have a passion for learning and love what they teach. They are lifelong learners, actively searching for new, enriching learning experiences.

- Inspiring teachers practice what they preach, one reason why students respect them.

- Inspiring teachers always respect students, never belittle them, or speak sarcastically in the classroom.

- Inspiring teachers conduct themselves professionally with students and avoid the "either-or" trap that saps energy unnecessarily. They are enthusiastic and expect students to work hard.

Equipped with extensive knowledge, a range of effective teaching skills, and engaging personal qualities, inspiring teachers create classrooms where both students and teachers thrive.

Reflect, Personalize, & Implement

Reflect
- What are some qualities of inspiring teachers?
- Do you agree that establishing a positive relationship with students is the most essential characteristic of an inspiring teacher?
- Identify other qualities of an inspiring teacher that were not identified in this chapter.

Personalize
- What inspiring characteristics do you already demonstrate?
- Think about teachers who inspired you. Identify the qualities that made them special to you.

Implement

- Identify at least one quality you would like to develop to help you become a more inspiring teacher.
- How will you use the information provided in this chapter to help you become a teacher who makes a positive difference in the lives of students?

CHAPTER 5

Inspiring Your Students

What can teachers do to inspire students and create a community of learners? Even the best classrooms can be challenging. With increased accountability, decreased funding, and too many disengaged students, teaching is more difficult than ever before. Despite the obstacles, when you create a learning environment compatible with brain-based learning and the principles of internal control psychology, and activate the internal motivation within your students, education is an exciting, need-satisfying process for everyone.

Building The Classroom Community

Education is based on human relationships. Only people can inspire students in great numbers. Used appropriately, technology enhances education, but technology can never inspire like a great teacher. A student already interested in a particular subject can be successful when the teaching relies primarily on technology. Given anything less than an interested student, technology cannot teach even reasonably well, much less inspire. That's why technology will never be more than an adjunct to the heart of the educational process: the interaction between teacher and student.

Take a moment right now and think about times you were asked to learn something that required hard work. If the task itself was important to you, the relationship between you and the person asking you to do the work was probably not critical. Even if you did not like the other person, you put forth effort because you valued the work. You were internally motivated to learn what was being taught.

If you had a positive relationship with the person asking you to work, the quality of your work was probably even higher. Your full emotional energy went into the task instead of being split between the satisfying work and the negative thoughts that characterize a poor relationship. You probably felt comfortable seeking the other person's help if you needed it. Even if you don't value a task initially, a positive relationship with a caring teacher increases the chances of you appreciating that what you're being asked to learn will add quality to your life.

Learning is a process of discovery. In a positive environment, we naturally want to learn more, share more, make new connections, and continue the exciting process of discovery. Research repeatedly suggests that kids learn more when they have a positive relationship with their teachers (Schaps, 2003, p. 31; Marzano, 2003, p. 6; Leachman and Victor, 2003, p. 67; Sullo, 2007, p. 28; Tate, 2004, p.32). If you want test scores to improve in your school, creating positive relationships between teachers and students should be a priority. By the same token, a negative environment can have dire consequences. When students feel threatened, their motivation, productivity, and achievement decline dramatically (Jensen 1995, 232). The psychological threat that accompanies sarcasm, criticism, and ridicule is as damaging as physical threat.

Inspiring teachers intentionally foster positive relationships with students from the outset. In some cases, that means starting even before the teacher and students are in the same classroom. For example, several teachers in my children's K-8 school learned the names of all the students in the school, greeting them in the corridors regardless of the grade or classroom they were in. When a seventh or eighth grade teacher says hello to younger students by name, the students feel important. When those students eventually get to the seventh or eighth grade, they are much less likely to be disruptive because students generally do not disrupt with adults who have treated them well. Moreover, they are likely to work harder because a positive relationship has already been established.

Some teachers I supervised as a middle school administrator sent letters to incoming students a few weeks before school began, telling the students a little about what they would study and the academic and behavioral expectations. The tone of the letter was positive and teachers made certain to personalize their letters in some way so students felt special when they received them. (Even young kids hate getting a form letter.) The reason why these letters were effective is that students felt a connection with the teacher even before they started the school year. A successful letter will leave students anticipating the start of a challenging year filled with exciting learning opportunities.

An administrative colleague of mine made it a point to know every student in our school even though he worked directly with only about a third of the students. Not surprisingly, he was more successful than any other adult in the building with disruptive students. Because he showed genuine interest in who they were and what mattered to them, they behaved appropriately in his presence and listened to his advice.

Some schools have incoming students visit their new building during a designated orientation or "step-up" day. Done well, the experience is a valuable first step in forging positive relationships with incoming students. Done poorly, it can be unproductive or even damaging. Students can feel scared, overwhelmed, and intimidated by the prospect of moving to the next level. Inspiring teachers keep things positive, knowing that the primary purpose of the experience is to have incoming students feel connected to their new school.

When well-meaning, but overbearing, adults caution incoming students about the rules and the consequences of violating them, the value of the experience is undermined. While this information may be important to communicate, stern warnings sorely compromise the objective: creating positive relationships with incoming students. We are better off saying we are looking forward to working and learning together, not intimidating students with admonitions of what will happen if they don't follow the school's rules. A successful orientation ends with incoming students excited about entering the school, not frightened of what will happen to them when they get there.

Start Out Right

Inspiring teachers know exactly what they want from their students and themselves on the first day of school. They aren't doing things on the fly. Here are some ideas about how to begin the school year positively and productively:

- Since you want students consistently producing high quality academic work, the classroom must be non-threatening. It's important for students to perceive the classroom as a place where they can take risks, make mistakes, and grow. In a fear-laden environment, you may get compliance. There may be few disruptions. Students may perform reasonably well on evaluations that require only superficial thinking. But you will never get their best work.

- Let kids know right away that you have no interest in punishing. Your sole objective is to teach. Tell them you expect they will work hard and they will sometimes struggle academically. Academic struggles communicate that students are actively engaged and trying to master concepts. Tell them that confusion, struggle, and frustration indicate that they are moving forward.

- Put learners in the best position to persevere and achieve. Help them view academic struggles positively and move from thinking, "I'm frustrated. I don't get this" toward, "I'm frustrated. If I keep working, I can learn this even though it's difficult. This is pretty exciting." The reality reflected in the second statement is as valid as the first and fosters greater academic achievement.

The Class Vision

If you hope to inspire your students to achieve to their potential, you must have a shared vision of a quality classroom experience. On the first day of school, ask students to imagine that the school year (or the course) is over. The class was even better than they hoped. They learned a tremendous amount of useful information. Remind them that your goal is academic. You want everyone to enjoy themselves, but your primary objective is educational. Have students keep the academic mission of the class in mind as they visualize. Have them describe what they learned and what they did that led them to say, "This class was great!"

Have students put their ideas in writing because it increases the chances of them taking responsibility and doing their part to ensure that the class is successful. When everyone has finished, discuss what they each visualized. Participate in the activity, making sure that their vision includes all the elements essential for a successful class. The composite vision you create should identify to the students what a great class sounds like and looks like and what you would never hear and never see.

Once the class has created their vision of a quality classroom, talk with them about what they must do to achieve what they want. This helps students see that success is not simply provided by the teacher, but something they all contribute to. For a detailed, step-by-step description of how to create a shared vision with your students, I encourage you to read "Beyond Goals: creating An Inspiring Classroom." (Sullo).

Teacher's Job... Student's Job

"People need role clarification to do quality work" (Gossen and Anderson 1995, 40). After completing the class vision, define roles within the classroom. Explain that it's important for everyone to fully understand the teacher's job and the students' job. When they know exactly what they are expected to do, they have a better chance of being successful.

Using language that matches your style and personality, say something like this to your students: "To make this the great class we all want it to be, we need to figure out what each of us should do. We all have responsibilities, and it's important to identify exactly what your job is and what my job is. It's also important that we identify what is not my job and what is not your job. We are doing this so that we can work well together and have the best possible learning experience."

Create a chart with your students that looks like this:

Teacher's Job Is:	Student's Job Is:
Teacher's Job Is Not:	Student's Job is Not:

Post the "Teacher's Job...Student's Job" in a prominent place in the room. Referencing it is a simple, efficient way to remind students of their role in the classroom. A lot of times, when students get off task or engage in unwanted behavior, it's because they momentarily forget their "job" and get caught up in an interesting distraction. Rather than getting drawn into a power struggle, simply remind the students of their job in the classroom.

Many teachers reference the "Teacher's Job...Student's Job" after kids return from physical education or the cafeteria. It's not unusual for students to enter the room in a boisterous fashion, not in the most appropriate state for learning. A quick and positive "Remember what we need to do to make this a great class" while pointing to the "Teacher's Job...Student's Job" can help students quickly transition into a state more conducive to the high quality academic work you want.

Class Rules

Even in the best classrooms, there will be some inappropriate behavior. Careful development of classroom rules helps make managing disruption considerably easier. I don't believe I've ever met a teacher who doesn't have some rules.

Most educators agree that it is wise to involve students in formulating rules. As I say in workshops, if there is ever a revolution in the United States, it won't begin in Congress. Lawmakers don't revolt. Most students will disrupt on occasion – that's part of being a kid - but there will not be a revolution if they are genuinely involved in creating the rules. Just as democratic societies periodically amend their Constitution, students may want to amend classroom rules, but they will work within the system if they are given a voice.

When I was a classroom teacher, I created rules with my students. Hindsight being 20/20, I now can see a serious flaw in what I did. Once we had come to consensus about rules, I would say, "These are the rules we have agreed to. Can everybody live with them?" At the time, I had no idea that I was sending the following subliminal message: "I know rules are a nuisance and none of us like them, but can you tolerate them?" Rules, I implied, were a necessary evil.

Today, I would do things differently. I would still involve the students in developing the rules. I would make sure that things I value were included. Once we had compiled a list, I would have the class combine ideas so we had as few rules as possible. The fewer rules there are, the easier it is for everyone to remember them. (Plus, the classroom will feel less like a prison and more like the positive learning environment you are trying to create.)

While some may think that asking students to distill a huge list into a few general rules is a waste of valuable academic time, in truth it is a valuable activity that involves editing, summarizing, discriminating, and negotiating.

Finally, it's important for students to positively value the classroom rules. I would no longer say, "Can you live with these?" I want students to be thinking, "These rules are good for us, and we're glad we have them. If we behave according to these rules, we'll enjoy ourselves and learn more." Students who appreciate rules are more likely to internalize them and follow them even when they are not being watched.

As a middle school administrator, it was important to me that students behaved in an orderly way that supported learning. Each year, I visited classrooms and told kids that regardless of the individual classroom rules they developed, I expected them to include these three:

- Be safe

- Be respectful

- Be productive

We discussed what "safe, respectful, and productive" looked like and sounded like in the classroom. We talked about why these rules were important and agreed that we'd all have a more enjoyable school year if they followed these rules. My objective was clear: I wanted the students to value the rules and see them positively - not as annoyances to be endured. While there were occasional disruptions in our school, they were few and far between because we took time to discuss the positive nature of rules with the students.

Class Constitution

My friend and colleague Jon Erwin (2004, 101) suggests creating a class constitution with students rather than relying exclusively on classroom rules. By developing a class constitution, students feel powerful and are more likely to behave in a respectful manner.

Erwin's description of the process includes students identifying specific behaviors and attitudes they would like to see in the classroom. Working in small groups to maximize participation, they create their vision of a quality classroom and share them with the whole class. Once differences are resolved, the constitution is adopted and committed to by all members of the class.

Erwin finds that creating a class constitution works with students of all ages, results in fewer disruptions, and leads to increased academic achievement. I have helped many classes create constitutions and the students enjoy the process and seem committed to making their classroom an enjoyable, productive academic environment.

The First Day "Test"

While serious academic work begins immediately in a quality classroom, the initial focus is on creating a positive learning environment because this leads to greater academic achievement as the school year unfolds.

When he was a high school English teacher, Erwin gave his students a 20-question test on the first day of school (2004, 51). It included questions like the following:

- How long have I been a teacher?

- What are three things I do for fun?

- How many brothers and sisters do I have?

- What kind of music do I enjoy?

- Where did I grow up?

These questions created a positive atmosphere for learning and the kids left class the first day seeing Erwin as more than just "the English teacher." Their expanded perception created an environment where disruption was less likely.

As a follow-up, Erwin had students create tests about themselves. When students corrected them, they learned some interesting things about each other, breaking down long-held stereotypes and cliques while creating a supportive classroom.

Get to Work!

I encourage teachers to initiate activities related to the subject matter being studied as soon as school begins. Don't spend much time on activities that are unrelated to academics. If you dedicate excessive time to team-building, connecting activities during the first few days of school and only later introduce academic work, students may get the idea that connecting and learning are separate. Inspiring teachers don't want students wondering, "Are we learning or are we having fun?" They want students having fun while learning. There is no "either-or" dichotomy in the inspiring classroom.

Some years ago, I worked with a school that had a two-teacher team with a lot of discipline problems. At first, I thought they had a particularly difficult group of kids, something that happens from time to time. The teachers readily admitted, however, that their students were no more challenging than those on any other team and that poor behavior had plagued them for several years in a row. What they found most frustrating, they said, was that they spent the entire first week of school foregoing academics, immersing themselves in community-building activities. Since they "gave up" - their term - five full days to create a sense of connection with their students, they couldn't understand why the students would ever disrupt!

What these teachers had done was to cultivate an initial perception that school was all about play and connecting. By ignoring academics, they unwittingly devalued the very thing we care most about in school: student learning! Compounding the problem was the fact that these teachers did virtually nothing after the first week of school to maintain the feeling of connection and community on their team. When I asked why, they said, "We did that the first week," unaware that a positive classroom environment must be nurtured over time. Because I had a long-term relationship with these teachers, we were able to devise a way for them to introduce serious academic work in an enjoyable way from the outset and to sustain a positive learning community. Not surprisingly, the disruptions decreased, the learning improved, and the teachers enjoyed their jobs a lot more.

At the beginning of the school year, inspiring teachers are less concerned about academic outcomes and more concerned about work habits, pride in academics, and how well the students interact with each other. They take note of students' achievement, but they are initially more interested in the following:

- Do students work diligently?

- Are students committed to quality?

- If some students are struggling, do others offer help, or is the classroom characterized by a "survival of the fittest" mentality?

- Are students a unified group, or are there cliques and isolates within the group?

Inspiring teachers know that these issues play a key role in how much learning will occur throughout the year.

Once a positive learning environment has been established, it must be maintained but energy can be focused on student learning and achievement. In a positive learning community, learning is sustained by internal motivation, peer support, and a classroom where effort and achievement are the rule, not the exception.

Everybody Is Important

The inspiring teacher values each student and genuinely believes everybody has something positive to contribute to the class. In too many schools, classes are already stratified. Some students are identified as "winners," those who are school-smart or play the school game well. Others are "losers," the disconnected students who rarely do quality work and frequently disrupt the learning of others. In the middle is a large group that could go either way. As classes become more diverse and students previously educated in separate settings are placed in regular education classes, minimizing potentially destructive stratification becomes increasingly important.

Create classrooms where all students are valued and contribute positively to the group. This starts by believing that everyone is valuable and has something to contribute, regardless of who they are or if they have an educational handicap. Students who are valued – not patronized – and are given a challenging, manageable environment do their best work. All students who put forth their best effort and make academic gains feel good about themselves as learners and appreciate the opportunity to contribute positively to the class.

Inspiring teachers aren't naive. They don't believe that all students learn in the same way or that all students will learn the same amount. They aren't magicians or miracle workers, but they do believe that all students can learn. Inspiring teachers help students achieve their learning potential by creating a classroom where all learners feel valued.

How do you do this? Words alone will not convince them. Older students in particular have heard such words for years. Students need actions demonstrating that you really believe in them. Here are some ideas to help create a learning environment where students feel valued.

Mismatchers

Some students learn most easily by searching for differences, exceptions, and discrepancies (Jensen 1995, 259). This group is called mismatchers because they learn by identifying what doesn't fit. While matchers look for similarities, mismatchers look for what violates the norm.

Matchers are generally managed easily in traditional classroom settings because they tend to agree and conform. Mismatchers are likely to argue and point out discrepancies. Like matchers, they are simply sorting through information in a way that is meaningful to them but teachers who don't appreciate this learning style can easily perceive mismatchers as disruptive and difficult. In reality, mismatchers who argue are not being disruptive or disrespectful. Arguing is evidence that the material actively engages them. They are just trying to put it together in a way that works for them – mismatching.

Some years ago I conducted a multi-day workshop for a school. The principal told me in advance that the group was generally positive but that one teacher was difficult and would challenge everything presented in the workshop. He was right. Fortunately, I knew about mismatchers and realized that this teacher was only trying to make sense of what was what was being discussed in the workshop. Because I was not offended by his learning style, he became an asset to the group. I helped his peers appreciate that he had something valuable to offer. Because the mismatcher felt valued, he only spoke when he had something useful to add. He was not driven to speak constantly to be acknowledged. The rest of the staff left the workshop better able to take advantage of his considerable wisdom, which they had largely ignored before. As the facilitator, I was pleased I had modeled how to include a mismatcher.

Introverts

Some students are extroverts. Others will naturally be more quiet and timid. In an inclusive classroom, every student is invited to participate, but not every student is expected to participate in the same way. If students are afraid to speak up because they may be criticized, ridiculed, or belittled, something is wrong. On the other hand, it's normal for some students to be quieter than others. Some students learn more by watching and internally processing as they make meaning. Accept and appreciate different learning styles, ensuring that students contribute in ways that maximize their learning. Quieter students are never penalized because of their learning style in a quality classroom.

Of course, verbal participation is an essential component of some classes, including foreign language classes. When regular verbal participation is necessary to ensure academic progress, make sure students understand why it's important. Students who perceive the importance of something are more likely to cooperate. Some students find presentations in front of the class more challenging, and inspiring teachers create an environment where learners are willing to risk stepping out of their comfort zones. In the right setting, most students will try something new.

It's important to determine why a student is quiet. If it's simply their style and personality, do everything possible to allow the student to learn, participate, and demonstrate competence in nonverbal ways. On the other hand, if a student wants to participate more actively but lacks skills, make the classroom a safe, inviting place and ensure the student is taught necessary skills. In some cases, a student may profit from working with a guidance counselor or other specialist to develop their social skills.

Cooperative Learning Groups

Cooperative learning groups can enhance inclusion in a classroom. Regularly changing group composition minimizes the chance of cliques forming and the class develops more cohesion. You can't just put students in groups and expect them to work well together. They need to be taught specific skills and their responsibilities must be carefully delineated.

Less experienced teachers sometimes think students walk into class with group skills in place. They quickly discover that students often have no idea about how to work effectively and responsibly in a group. Powerful students may bully others. A few students may do most, if not all, of the work while their partners freeload.

Minimal quality learning takes place and the teacher may decide that cooperative learning groups are a waste of time.

Inspiring teachers are less naive. Before directly teaching group skills, they discuss the value of group learning, building a shared vision with students. Then they teach students how to function effectively as a group and identify specific roles and responsibilities. (For group learning strategies, see Johnson, Johnson, and Holubec 1993; and Kagan, 1994).

Because complex challenges are most successfully met when approached with several kinds of intelligence, cooperative learning teams that reflect the diversity of talents represented in heterogeneous classes can be quite successful. Inspiring teachers let students know that every group needs the positive contributions of all members. As a result, every student feels valued and experiences the satisfaction that comes from putting forth effort and creating something of quality.

Emphasize Learning More Than Grades

Another way to build an environment where students feel valued is to emphasize learning rather than grades and uniform achievement. Regardless of standards and the push for high achievement, it's foolish to expect all students will achieve at a relatively equal rate. The abilities of typical students can vary by as much as three years within any one grade (Jensen 1995, 12). That doesn't even take into account the exceptional students who sit in virtually every classroom. Since typical students develop at such different rates, their acquisition of skills will naturally vary significantly. When we emphasize test scores and grades, we create competitive environments where some students are winners and others are losers. Typically, the losers withdraw or disrupt. The inspiring teacher does everything possible to avoid this.

Instead of emphasizing test scores and grades, focus on your fundamental mission: teaching. Keep students focused on their job: to learn as much as possible. Regardless of their relative strengths and weaknesses, all students can do their best and learn as much as possible. When kids understand their job and know they will not be compared with others, they are more likely to become the inspired students we want them to be.

A Passion for Teaching & Learning

I've emphasized the importance of interpersonal relationships because without supportive relationships we can't inspire large numbers of students to do quality work. But teachers must also have an enthusiasm for their subject matter.

One thing inspiring teachers share is a love of learning and a passion for the subjects they teach. While enthusiasm may not necessarily be contagious, boredom is deadly. Teachers who do not communicate excitement, joy in learning, and passion about what they teach will never inspire. They extinguish the spark to learn that students bring to school. Those who inspire show learners that what they are studying is interesting, stimulating, and worth working hard to learn.

The next time a student says, "Why would anyone want to learn this?" remember that you are probably dealing with a mismatcher who is giving you an opportunity to explain why your professional life is worthwhile. Explain why your subject matter is worth the student's attention, time, and effort. Identifying the importance of what you teach is more inspiring than saying, "Because you need it to graduate" or, "It's on the test." The issue is simple: Are you willing to settle for students who satisfy graduation requirements or do you want inspired learners who are excited about lifelong learning?

Make Lessons Relevant

"One of the best ways for students to deepen their learning about a particular concept or process is for them to see how it relates to their lives" (Erwin 2004, 90). If you want students to remember what you teach, make it relevant (Jensen 1995, 110).

Creating relevant work does not need to be cumbersome or time consuming. I worked with a math teacher who put her students' names in the word problems she created. That simple strategy engaged the students significantly more than if the same problem came directly from the text. That same teacher did an activity around the holidays where students were given a set amount of imaginary money and used advertising fliers to "buy" gifts. The goal was to spend as close to the allotted budget as possible. Students were given additional credit if they calculated the sales tax. As I watched the students complete this activity, it was evident they were engaged by the task, developed their skills, and enjoyed themselves because the lesson was meaningful to them.

Most students in the middle school where I worked liked sports. During football season, one teacher used the score of the New England Patriots football game to review mean, median, mode, and range. Simply because it related to something the kids enjoyed, they looked forward to a weekly review and brush-up of essential math skills.

As a former English teacher, I value the importance of writing and want students to express themselves clearly and with precision. Some of the best writing I saw from our 5th grade students was when they shared essays with me about why we should bring back outdoor recess, extend lunchtime, and hold dances for the younger students. When students are given topics that are meaningful to them, they suddenly appreciate why it's important to have a strong introduction, substantive arguments, supporting detail, and a strong conclusion. When they know their papers are going to be read by a school administrator, they want to have correct spelling, format, and mechanics so their thoughts will be taken more seriously.

As I observed classrooms on a daily basis, I frequently asked the teacher how the students could use what was being taught. I didn't do that to put teachers on the spot. I was trying to make sure that students saw the relevance of what they were learning. When students know how they can use something, they are more likely to commit time and energy to learn it well.

Meaningful Homework

There is considerable debate about the value of homework. Studies can be found suggesting that homework is of little value, perhaps even counterproductive. Other studies suggest that homework is essential and students benefit from the opportunity to practice skills.

Regardless of your feelings about homework, one thing is certain: homework has no value unless students do it. Too many teachers assign homework that is not completed by the majority of students. The result is unprepared students who typically disrupt the class. Once that cycle begins, it's hard to break.

If the success of your next lesson is contingent upon students completing their homework, you are giving up control of the class. If you decide to assign homework, make sure that tomorrow's learning is not compromised by those students who choose not to do it.

Students are more likely to do homework when they perceive it as relevant. Asking students who earn a perfect score on a spelling pre-test to write each spelling word five times is foolish, yet it is done in countless classes in the name of "responsibility and accountability." Is it any wonder students rebel against assignments that are patently absurd?

If you must assign homework, be sure it is meaningful and explain to students why it is important. Ask students if spending time working independently at home will help them achieve the academic goals they have set. How will doing the assignment enhance learning? Teachers should know the answer to that question before giving any assignment. (If you can't figure out why doing the assignment is important, why would you expect a kid to take it seriously – or do it at all?)

An argument can be made that performance improves with practice. If that's true for the subject you teach, help your students appreciate that doing homework is valuable. In numerous conversations with non-performing students, they tell me they don't do homework because "it's stupid" or "a waste of time." When they see it as something valuable, even reluctant learners are more likely to complete work at home.

If your goal is to help students develop a work ethic and responsibility, assign something that each student can successfully complete regardless of their skill or ability. Every student can read an independent book for so many minutes a night even if they can't all read the same number of pages or comprehend at the same level. Every student can self-assess and identify an area where they would profit from focused review and practice for so much time each night. Many teachers tell me their primary objective in assigning homework is to foster a sense of responsibility. Assignments that increase the student's skill and knowledge base are more likely to be completed and help in the development of a work ethic and a sense of responsibility.

Frustrated because too many students did not complete homework regularly, or did it but ended up disliking school and learning, Shea, Madden, and Shea (1997) developed "Create Your Own

Homework" to make homework useful and relevant. "Create Your Own Homework" balances freedom and structure. Students complete a homework project each week. The teachers suggest categories of inquiry to encourage varied learning activities, such as writing, reading, analyzing data, and doing calculations. After students finish their homework assignment, they fill out a self-evaluation form, outlining what they learned and how they can demonstrate their learning to peers.

What do parents think about this departure from the traditional homework routine? Most are supportive and grateful. They see their children completing homework assignments with enthusiasm, sometimes for the first time ever. Parents are delighted that their children are eager to do more than what is required and enjoy learning. "Create Your Own Homework" is an effective strategy that inspires quality. To many parents, it seems like a miracle.

Teaching Internal Control

If you teach any subject involving human interaction, you can teach your students about internal control and motivation. Some years ago, an English teacher asked me to help teach her students these concepts, but wanted it to flow naturally from her lesson. She didn't want to teach it separately at the expense of her primary role as an English teacher. She invited me to visit her class for a day.

I spent a few minutes with the students defining responsible behavior. We all agreed that responsible behavior means acting to satisfy our needs without interfering with others' attempts to satisfy theirs. It also needs to be safe and legal. I then introduced the four psychological basic needs: connecting/belonging, power, freedom, and fun. The entire teaching component took no more than 15 minutes.

The students had read the first half of the novel *The Pigman* by Paul Zindel and together we listed behaviors that the three main characters had already engaged in. I broke the class into learning teams and their task was to discuss what need or needs the behaviors had satisfied. (Remember, all our behavior is purposeful and is intended to satisfy our basic needs). It was exciting to listen to students arguing about what need a behavior addressed. Students then decided whether behaviors were responsible or less responsible and provided reasons for their decisions. What followed was a lively discussion about motivation and responsibility.

In any subject involving human interaction, it is easy to help students relate behaviors to basic needs, motivation, and responsibility. In this way, inspiring teachers can engage in fruitful discussion with students without feeling as if they are sacrificing time.

Beyond Cliques: The Caring Community of Learners

We are social beings. The need to connect drives us to seek companionship. We also have a need for safety and security which sometimes leads us to shut others out. It is common for any large group to include a number of subgroups. Individuals feel secure within one subgroup but may hesitate to make connections outside it.

In classrooms, this tendency manifests in the formation of cliques, groups that satisfy the needs for belonging and security. In some schools, cliques are arenas where the need for power is also met, often irresponsibly. For example, many gangs threaten other kids or engage in violent behavior, providing their members tremendous power.

Inspiring teachers don't pretend there aren't cliques or gangs. Instead, they relentlessly focus on their mission: to have students learn as much as possible and develop skills that will help them live responsibly and make a contribution to their community. As long as teachers actively reach out to everyone, nearly every student will see the value of school. Because we have a need to be competent, all students want to develop skills that will give them recognition within their community. Students who do not get positive recognition in school are more likely to seek it elsewhere, including gangs.

Inspiring teachers work with their students to develop a shared quality world vision of a classroom where all students are included, even those unable to express themselves effectively. They help students see that they are more powerful and better off when everyone in the class is involved and positively connected with one another. Most students can't create this vision independently because they lack the skills to envision an inclusive, inviting community of learners.

Some kids are so frightened of moving outside their comfort zone that they will resist and ridicule your efforts, at least initially. They may mask their fear with bravado, but inspiring teachers do not give up easily. They know they succeed only when they build a group that incorporates and transcends the subgroups within the class.

Of course, kids will continue to be more attracted to some of their peers and less attracted to others. Such behavior is natural and acceptable. Still, breaking down barriers helps all students experience more satisfaction in school.

Never challenge the value and legitimacy of the groups to which students already belong. Instead of breaking up cliques, help students develop an additional quality world picture that embodies the whole class. Outside the class, students may drift back to their original cliques where they find the safety, security, belonging, and power they seek. All those needs, however, can be satisfied within the inspiring classroom when students become positively connected to the whole class. When teachers help students discover that important fact, they can create a supportive, caring community of learners with relative ease.

Summary

Inspiring teachers create classrooms where students regularly produce quality work. The most important step is forging positive working relationships with all students. Help students see themselves as members of a learning community. A positive learning environment is created so students will do their best work.

Inspiring teachers work collaboratively with students to clarify roles and responsibilities in the classroom. They provide relevant and meaningful learning opportunities so students give their best effort. Inspiring teachers and their students develop a shared vision of a quality classroom, knowing this vision will motivate students to achieve academically and behave responsibly.

Inspiring teachers employ practices that promote high achievement, such as well-structured cooperative learning groups. They ensure that all students, even those frequently misunderstood, are valued and included in the learning community. Fueled by a love of learning and a passion for the subjects they teach, inspiring teachers create classrooms where students are encouraged to explore, challenge themselves, and grow academically and socially.

Reflect, Personalize, & Implement

Reflect

- Identify and describe some of the most valuable ideas presented in this chapter.

- What are some specific things you can do at the beginning of the school year to create a classroom environment that supports high achievement?
- Discuss why it is helpful to identify roles and responsibilities within a classroom.

Personalize

- What do you do to create positive relationships with your students?
- What do you do to ensure that all students feel valued and included in your classroom?
- What do you do to help students see that what you teach is relevant and meaningful?

Implement

- What can you do to enhance relationships in your classroom so that students will achieve more?
- Identify something you will do to make learning meaningful and relevant to your students.
- If you assign homework, what will you do to make it a meaningful learning experience that students value?

CHAPTER 6

Inspiring Your Colleagues

Many teachers ask if they can positively influence their colleagues as well as their students. This chapter suggests ways for teachers to inspire their peers, creating the energy necessary for systemic change.

Don't Preach

When I conduct workshops to help teachers and schools increase their effectiveness, it's not unusual for participants to ask how they can influence their colleagues and implement change on a school-wide basis. As much as I like it when participants find my workshops valuable, their language often betrays their reliance on external control. They ask how they can *make* their colleagues see the value of what they have learned in the workshop, unaware that they are operating from a coercive, external control perspective. They say everyone *should* believe what they now believe, using language that would deny their peers a chance to evaluate ideas for themselves. Some speak as though they have discovered "the truth" – and feel obliged to share it with everyone, even those who may not want to – or be ready to - hear it.

When confronted by unchecked enthusiasm, I encourage participants to slow down and preserve relationships with colleagues who may not know what they know, and may not believe what they believe. Most of us dismiss colleagues who preach to us after they have a particularly meaningful learning experience. Unsolicited advice can be a thinly disguised form of criticism, something that destroys even the best relationships.

If you want to make sure that your colleagues never hear what you have to say, preach to them. Tell them you have found "the truth" and know how to inspire students. It won't take long for you to become an outcast in your building, largely ignored and unappreciated. You may have valuable ideas and information, but unless you present yourself less offensively, your information is useless. No one will listen. As my father used to say, albeit in somewhat less professional language, "No one likes a smartass."

So, what can you do?

Walk The Talk

If you want to have any chance of influencing your colleagues, be certain your actions match your words. Model the principles that inspire others. Be inviting and nonjudgmental with your colleagues. Above all, never offer advice unless asked. Go about your business and build strong relationships with your colleagues. Remember that we are multidimensional beings with lives that extend beyond the school and the world of education. Demonstrate the same interest in your colleagues that you do with your students. Communicate about ordinary experiences such as family, hobbies, weekend plans, vacations, illness, interests, and current events. If you talk to colleagues only about school and school-related issues, you only get to know a part of them, albeit an important part. When you develop a more complete connection, one that respects the boundaries each person wishes to maintain, you will undoubtedly talk about various issues that matter, including school.

Maintain Your Individuality

While inspiring teachers share many qualities, they are not all cut from the same cloth. This is the story of one of my son's teachers. Because they worked together many years ago, some of the "cutting edge" practices described in the following paragraphs have become somewhat common. While this teacher has since moved to another community, I suspect he will remain an inspiring teacher for as long as he teaches.

Dave Driscoll is a former marine. A large man with a booming voice, he has a presence that can intimidate adults and students alike. Dave organizes his classroom in a no-nonsense way that is more dictatorship than democracy. Students know his classroom is a place where hard work is expected and disruption is best avoided.

Above all else, Dave Driscoll is an inspiring teacher with a passion for learning. Students entering his classroom are bombarded with information. Learning is the objective and the sources of inspiration are many and varied. There is a reference section in the room. There are computers, many borrowed from colleagues who have not taken the time to incorporate them into the curriculum. There is Internet access, putting the most current information from around the world at the students' fingertips. There are posters around the room. Some have inspirational quotations about hard work, achievement, and the joy of persevering. Some are content related, providing information about a range of topics. No matter how inspiring the teacher and how relevant the subject matter, student eyes will wander. In Dave's classroom, drifting eyes encounter something worth learning.

My son Greg was fortunate enough to learn from Dave. Greg was a high-achieving student with the capacity to be disruptive, though not malicious. In Dave Driscoll's sixth grade class, disruptions were infrequent and easily managed, and the learning was high quality.

When I asked Greg what he valued most about Dave Driscoll, he said, "Mr. Driscoll is tough, but he's always fair." As a parent, I particularly remember one experience where Dave combined firmness and fairness to enhance Greg's learning.

Dave had given the students a math test to work on over several days. All of his tests were take-home, open-book test. He encouraged students to use whatever resources they had to solve the problems. Greg had never written down his assignments in a homework notebook. He saw no reason to put something in writing if could easily remember what and when an assignment was due.

Greg worked diligently on his math test and submitted it when he thought it was due, confident that he had done well. Dave asked if he wanted the test corrected.

"Of course," Greg answered. "Why are you asking?"

"Since you didn't turn it in when it was due," Dave said, "you won't receive any credit. I just want to know if you are still interested in feedback."

To some, this may sound harsh and punitive, but the most important perception is the student's. When I asked Greg what he thought, he said he knew the consequences for not turning in work on time. In his mind, the matter was handled fairly.

Dave called me to ask if I was comfortable with how he handled the situation. I had only one question: Would this impact Greg's math placement for the following school year? Dave assured me that receiving no credit for turning in a test after the due date would never adversely affect a student's placement. "I just want Greg to learn that it's wise to write down the assignment. No matter how good a memory you have," Dave said. That experience helped my son learn an important lesson.

In addition to a passion for teaching and a profound sense of fairness, Dave follows the principles of brain-based learning in his classroom. He adapts his teaching approach to what current research suggests is most effective. Textbooks are secondary in his classroom, resources to aid the teacher, not masters that drive the instruction. Finally, Dave has a clear sense of what he wants students to be able to do at the completion of a lesson or unit. While he provides options, demonstrating competence is non-negotiable.

We have all had special teachers, people who inspired us. Dave Driscoll was one of those teachers for my son and for many other students in our community. I am grateful that Greg had a chance to learn from this special teacher.

Creating & Sustaining Energy In Your Building

When you inspire students to do their best work, create need-satisfying classrooms, and build brain-friendly learning environments, it's exciting to share your success with others and feel supported during difficult times. If you are working to inspire students in your building or district, I suggest that you form a networking group to build and sustain energy. In many districts, your work can earn professional development credits. Working in isolation is exhausting and not as satisfying as being connected to a larger group committed to the same ideas.

Meet with like-minded colleagues to share strategies and successes and avoid the negative comments that can demoralize even the most committed teachers. Be certain that your meetings are open to all staff members. If meetings are by invitation only, you will be modeling elitism, clique building, and divisiveness. Your group will be nothing more than an irrelevant cohort that does little to positively impact the culture of the school.

When you improve the culture of a school, struggling schools become successful and successful schools become even better. No matter how effective any individual teacher may be, it takes a critical mass to sustain systemic change. That's the power of a networking group. Collective action can positively change the system.

How do you create a networking group? Ask your colleagues if they are interested in discussing how to inspire more students to work hard in school. There is interest in most schools. Many schools are repositories of latent energy waiting to be tapped. Lots of teachers are frustrated and would welcome a chance to talk about how to get more kids excited about learning. For the most part, however, teachers aren't invited to talk about what they think will work. Instead, they are subjected to sessions where outside experts tell them what they should be doing. If you agree with me that the current professional development model doesn't work especially well, maybe you can change it.

Teachers are understandably reluctant to give time to something that has no value. No one needs to waste time. Your colleagues need to believe that what you are suggesting will add quality to their lives. Experienced teachers will want to know how this group will be different from the other fads they have encountered over the years. We've all done too many "flavors of the month." Make sure they know that this has the potential to make a positive difference for their students. Emphasize that inspiring more kids to work hard and excel academically will make teaching more enjoyable. Some may be moved by comments about improved student achievement. Everyone, however, will be interested in learning how to enjoy their jobs more.

It is essential to get administrative approval for a formal networking effort. The ideal group will have administrative leadership, not simply approval. Waiting for such leadership, however, keeps you in the victim box, relying on others for things to change. In the words attributed to Gandhi: "You must be the change you want to see in the world" (1913). Be proactive once there is administrative approval for a group to begin meeting regularly, even if you have to run it yourself.

Any reasonable administrator will encourage discussions to help more students work hard and do better work. Any reasonable administrator will encourage discussions about how students learn most effectively. Any reasonable administrator will encourage staff to share successes and proven strategies so their collective wisdom is fully used and the culture of the school supports student growth and learning. If you proceed wisely, your administrator will likely approve a group – and perhaps even offer enthusiastic support.

How Do We Interact?

Diane Gossen and Judy Anderson (1995) identify three types of schools: the conventional school, the congenial school, and the collegial school. The conventional school is one where teachers are relatively autonomous and work in isolation. There is little or no sharing. Teachers tend to keep their doors closed and maintain a level of competition with each other. ("If I have a successful strategy, why would I share it with others? They might use it to get ahead of me.")

The congenial school is characterized by friendships, celebrations, and other social events. Because the emphasis is on getting along with others, teachers in the congenial school avoid conflict. Maintaining superficial harmony is the primary value, so contentious topics are avoided. When something controversial is brought up, teachers generally remain silent, although silent meetings are often followed by vibrant gossip sessions. Scott Peck (1988, 109) identifies this as a "pseudocommunity." Afraid that honest disagreement and conflict will damage relationships, members adopt a façade of congeniality while tension simmers just below the surface.

The collegial school is not afraid of conflict. Staff members believe that relationships are strengthened when they engage in vigorous, honest interactions instead of settling for superficiality in dialogue and relationships. The use of internal control psychology helps staff move to this level of interaction.

Inspiring teachers strive to build collegial schools. They accept differences, argue respectfully, and passionately engage in discussions about how to make classrooms and schools better. From my discussions with teachers around the world, I'm confident we are making steady progress away from conventional schools. Teachers are sharing more with one another and working more collaboratively. In candid moments, however, most teachers tell me that their schools are more congenial than collegial. To reach the next level of school improvement, we must create schools that are truly collegial, the most professional environment in which to conduct the important work of education.

Making Connections Beyond Your Building

Build and maintain energy by connecting with others outside your school or district. If you feel isolated in your building because others do not share your beliefs, connect with others around the country and the world engaged in the same pursuit as you.

Attend workshops and conferences and join organizations aimed at improving schools and inspiring academic achievement by implementing the ideas of internal control psychology and brain-based learning in developmentally appropriate ways. Professional learning opportunities help you continue learning while receiving affirmation that you are moving in a positive direction.

At the end of *The Inspiring Teacher* I have included a list of sites to help you connect with other educators striving to inspire quality.

It would be wonderful if your colleagues took advantage of all the innovative, effective ideas that are available. Some are bogged down with other commitments. Some simply don't care enough to vigorously pursue professional development. Inspiring teachers hope their colleagues decide to embark on a journey that will enhance their skills, but they won't be deterred by those who would maintain the status quo. Everyone is invited to learn together, but inspiring teachers are moving forward now. Another Gandhi quote: "We need not wait to see what others do" (1913, 241).

The Importance Of Administrative Leadership

It would be nice if inspiring teachers could succeed without strong leadership from administration. Of course, they *can* inspire their students even in a relatively coercive school with an unenlightened administrator – great teachers have been doing that for years. But to make a positive change in the culture of the school, teachers need strong leadership from building-level administrators.

If you work in a school that lacks supportive leadership, you have several options. One is to accept the situation and focus on your students and classroom. As long as you are satisfied by inspiring your students without effecting change on a larger scale, this option will work for you.

If you want your influence to extend beyond the door of your classroom, begin by garnering administrative support. The same qualities that inspire your students will help in this process. You need to build a positive working relationship with administration. This is an area where many inspiring teachers are horribly ineffective. They may be adept at forging strong working relationships with reluctant students, but they have great difficulty doing the same with reluctant administrators. Many get caught in the "they should know better" trap. This may be true, but it does nothing to improve the school. Remember this: everyone – including less-enlightened colleagues and administrators – is doing the best they can. If you believe you have something to offer administrators, if you hope to inspire them, begin building a positive working relationship. Anything less is counterproductive. Some administrators want to lead with energy, but they lack the skills and the courage. Let your administrators know that you want them to lead you on a journey that will make your school a better place to grow and learn.

A more extreme option, one requiring considerable thought, is to find another school. More schools are discovering that an emphasis on internal control and motivation results in increased student achievement. More administrators are finding that they satisfy the demands of those who cry for higher standards when they adopt an inspiring model and abandon the fundamentally flawed "carrot and stick" model. Moving to a new school is frightening, but for some it represents their best chance to build a meaningful, professionally satisfying career.

Summary

Many inspiring teachers want to influence their colleagues. The most helpful first step is to model what you espouse. Over time, some of your colleagues will want to know how they, too, can be more satisfied in their work and more successful with their students. As more teachers inspire students to do quality work consistently, professionals can share ideas and support one another. With leadership from administrators, inspiring teachers can collectively initiate long-lasting, systemic change and positively impact the culture of the school.

Reflect, Personalize, & Implement

Reflect
- What ideas do you think are most important to inspire your colleagues?
- Identify characteristics of the conventional, congenial, and collegial school.
- Give some examples of how you can maintain your individual style while being an inspiring teacher.

Personalize
- Would you characterize your school as conventional, congenial, or collegial? Why?
- What qualities do you possess that will help you inspire your colleagues?
- Are you satisfied with inspiring your students? Do you want to be part of a school where more teachers intentionally foster an environment that promotes high academic achievement in a joyful atmosphere?

Implement
- Identify at least one strategy you will use to inspire your colleagues. When will you start?
- What can you do to sustain your energy and stay focused on your goal of inspiring students?

CHAPTER 7

Forging an Alliance with Parents

Quality public education is a cornerstone of a democratic society. More and more parents are frustrated today with public schools and public school teachers. As a result, increasing numbers of students are being enrolled in private schools or are being home educated. Charter schools – public schools unencumbered by many of the rules governing traditional public schools – are gaining popularity.

The number abandoning traditional public schools is growing and our social structure will be forever changed if we do not take effective action quickly. If parents continue to seek alternative forms of education, we will create a de facto class system. Parents with financial means will understandably give their children an educational experience perceived to be superior to that offered by a decimated public school system. Public school graduates will be at a distinct disadvantage when it's time to apply to college or seek employment. Pay and other markers of respect will go disproportionately to a smaller elite. The concept of a meritocracy and an equal playing field regarding education will be nothing more than a memory.

For democracy to flourish, there must be a public school system that provides a quality education for the vast majority and equality of opportunity for all. A small minority have always been educated separately and given advantages unavailable to the mass-

masses. As long as their numbers remain small, a public school system remains a viable part of society.

Parents are one of our most valuable and least valued resources. Educators need to reengage parents who have lost faith in public education and public educators. If we want to bring parents back, they must see us as experts in the field and have confidence that their children will get a quality education in our schools. Nothing less will do.

What Went Wrong?

Why is it that so many parents don't trust us, think that we are ill-prepared to teach their children, and turn in desperation to educational alternatives? In answering these questions, it is not important whether the perceptions of parents are accurate. If parents believe that public educators in traditional public schools are less committed and competent than teachers in other settings, they will act based on that perception.

To save our public schools, we need to create a strong alliance with parents characterized by mutual respect and support. Currently, we don't have one and parents in increasing numbers are listening to those who hold us in low regard. We must regain the trust and support of our constituents.

Intimidation

Too many parents are intimidated by schools, teachers, and a system they don't fully understand. Often, we contact parents only when there is a problem. Although this occurs at every level, it is especially common in secondary schools. Secondary school teachers have so many students they argue it is difficult to have regular, positive contact with parents. When there is a problem, however, teachers almost always find the time to contact the home.

Not surprisingly, when parents are contacted by the school, their first thought is often, "What's wrong?" Why do parents typically jump to the conclusion that there must be something wrong if the school is contacting them? Because too often that has been their experience. Of course, they are likely to be defensive and cautious. Think of all the calls you have made as a professional to the homes of your students. Were calls made because of problems or were you just as likely to call when things were going well?

Most teachers tell me that the vast majority of their calls are generated by academic or behavioral concerns. They are quick to point out that they have too many students and not enough time to call unless there is a serious problem. Even if that point is valid, it doesn't build positive relationships with parents. Explaining a problem is not the same as solving it.

How do you want parents to perceive you and the school? Does your behavior – only calling them when there is a problem – help you build positive, supportive relationships with parents? If parents perceived school-initiated contact less negatively, it would be easier to create the positive relationship we want. There are a number of ways to improve the situation.

Positive Contacts

There are teachers who make positive phone contact with the parents of all of their students. To keep the conversations brief, they let parents know when they call that they have only a few minutes. The tone of each conversation is professional but light, and the focus is on affirming that both the teacher and parent want the child to be successful. Among other things, they discuss how to support each other as two important influences in the student's life. The goal is to build a partnership, not create an adversarial relationship.

It's hard to overstate the value of such conversations. Parents appreciate you taking time to contact them because you want their child to experience success and they will support you as the year unfolds. If you need to contact them later because of a problem, the positive history you have established will help you work collaboratively. Instead of being defensive, the parents will be inclined to resolve issues without rancor.

Secondary teachers often have student loads that make phone contact with each parent burdensome. There are ways to manage this situation. When students are grouped into teams, for example, teachers can share the responsibility, calling only the parents of students in their homeroom. During the conversations, teachers can indicate that all teachers on the team want to work collaboratively with parents.

If phone conversations are too time-consuming, an e-mail or letter to parents can be effective. Remember that the objective is to build an alliance with parents. Refrain from including anything extraneous. Keep your written communication brief and personalize it as much as possible. Communicating that you care about their child will never hurt your relationship, and it has the potential to help significantly.

Parent Conferences

School conferences are frightening experiences for many parents. I have attended countless meetings that included 6 to 10 professional educators and one parent. Imagine what it feels like to be the parent, especially since parent conferences are often held because of some difficulty a student is experiencing. The parent sits in a room full of professionals who are in a familiar environment among colleagues. The educators have the luxury of professional distance and detachment, while the parent is quite literally discussing their kid, their flesh and blood. You may all be sharing same space, but you certainly aren't sharing the same experience.

Like all of us, parents want to feel competent. Under these conditions, parents will act to protect against their discomfort. Some get aggressive, blaming and criticizing the school. Some berate their child in an effort to develop an alliance with the teachers. Some sit silently, almost numb, waiting only for the meeting to end. Regardless, it's hard to imagine a successful conference in these circumstances.

How can you make these meetings less intimidating and more collaborative? First, limit the number of staff at the meeting. Only invite staff members who are essential. Second, include at least one staff member with whom the parent has a positive, trusting connection. Third, the person who facilitates the meeting should articulate the following at the outset: the purpose of the meeting is to help the student be successful in school. Any comments that support the objective are welcome. Anything else, including blaming and arguing, is discouraged.

Some schools designate a staff member to act as a parent advocate at meetings. This person intentionally listens to comments from the likely perspective of the parent. This staff member asks questions that a timid parent might fear asking or that an uninformed parent might not think to ask. This assures that potential parental concerns are discussed.

Fear

Fear is a significant barrier to quality. When we are afraid, we automatically revert to primitive behaviors designed to protect us. The brain shifts to survival mode (Howard 1994, 259). Blood rushes to the large muscles, those most essential when the choice is fight or flight. With most of the oxygenated blood rushing to the large muscles, the brain experiences a decrease in blood, oxygen, and other nutrients. The frontal lobes, the end point in the circulation route, suffer first and most when we feel threatened. The frontal lobes are responsible for long-range thinking, problem solving, and higher-level thinking skills. If we want productive meetings with parents, fear is counterproductive.

Many parents are afraid of school personnel because of their own school experiences. Even though this is not our fault, inspiring teachers appreciate this and do everything possible to minimize fear when working with parents. It is not enough to say, "We understand it's hard for you to discuss your child's difficulty in school. We want to collaborate so that your child can be a successful student." Parents must leave the meeting believing that we really did work together for the benefit of their child if they are to trust us. We must choose our words carefully, mean what we say, and deliver on any promises that we make. When we have built a reputation as people who mean what we say and who work with parents for the betterment of students, parents will trust us more and fear us less.

Don't Condescend

At the beginning of my workshops, I frequently ask teachers what behaviors they find bothersome in a workshop leader. They usually say, "Don't be condescending. We can't stand it when a presenter talks down to us. If you do that, we won't learn much from you."

Parents are no different. When we talk down to them, they turn us off. We lose any chance of building a collaborative relationship with them.

There are many ways to be condescending. Some professionals enjoy using educational jargon that confuses anyone outside the field. Sometimes the condescending behaviors are more subtle, involving tone of voice, body language, and when and how people are acknowledged. To determine if your approach is appropriate, ask yourself, "If I were the parent at this meeting, would I feel like a valued member of the team, someone who is respected as much as everyone else at the table, or would I feel trivialized, patronized, and put up with because I must be tolerated?" Your answer will help you determine what to do next.

Parents Care

One of the most unproductive perceptions we can develop is, "These parents just don't care." Unfortunately, I have heard it said too often over the years. In nearly 40 years of working in public education, I have encountered many parents with poor parenting skills, but I have not met one about whom I would say, "This parent doesn't care."

Whether we are talking about effective parents or ineffective parents, well-educated parents or poorly educated parents, financially well-off parents or economically disadvantaged parents, couples or single parents, all of them want their kids to be successful. They may not have the skill to demonstrate their desire clearly, or we may not be skilled enough to see it, but all parents care about their children.

Inspiring teachers ask, "Does it help me to see some parents as uncaring? Would it be more helpful and just as accurate to see parents as caring but unskilled in some way or uninformed about something I think is important?" The latter approach helps you view parents more favorably, work more comfortably with them, and maintain a positive role: to provide skills and information that will help parents become more effective.

Difficult Parents

Education is a unique profession. Other professions are often shrouded in mystery and practitioners are less subject to criticism because what they do is alien to their constituents. For instance, few patients believe they know enough medicine to question their doctor, and most clients trust that their attorney knows more about law than they do. In contrast, many parents see themselves as educational experts – I guess because they went to school - and don't hesitate to question a teacher's expertise.

Although parents like this are easily seen as meddlesome and problematic, inspiring teachers choose to perceive parents in a way that lets them do their jobs more effectively. They realize that all parents – even annoying ones - want their kids to be successful. They understand that an aggressive, inappropriate presentation by a parent often masks underlying fears and insecurities. It may be a bitter pill to swallow, but even difficult parents are doing the best they can.

Regardless of how parents act, inspiring teachers remain focused on building and maintaining a positive working relationship for the benefit of students. Identifying areas of agreement with parents and forging a shared vision is the most effective way to deal with all parents, including those who can be difficult.

The most difficult and vocal parents can become our biggest allies precisely because they're so energetic and passionate. Our job is to educate them so that they voice their opinions loudly and strongly in support of what we are doing. Until we develop positive relationships with difficult parents, they will remain formidable adversaries rather than valuable allies.

Creating Parent and Community Support

Educators often bemoan the fact that parents and the community don't support them, especially when voters decide not to provide the funding necessary to maintain or enhance programs.

It's easy to criticize and blame an unsupportive community and wallow in collective frustration and anger. It's more productive to ask, "What have we done or failed to do that parents and the community don't support us the way we'd like?" In almost every case you will find a fractured relationship with parents and the community. We have failed to convince taxpayers that spending money on education is important. Instead of remaining mired in unproductive complaining, engage the public by forging an alliance with the community and build better relationships.

I usually avoid making analogies between education and business because what occurs in schools is very different from what occurs in commercial enterprises. In this case, however, a business comparison may be appropriate. Parents and the voting community represent our customers. Would any business be successful if it treated customers with as little regard as we sometimes treat parents and the community? At times, we forget who funds us and who we work for. We owe parents respect and courtesy. It's not only the right thing to do; it's the smart thing to do.

Charter schools have not made this mistake and that is one reason why they are increasingly popular with parents. Even though studies repeatedly suggest that the academic experience offered in charter schools is not substantially different from that offered in traditional public schools, more and more parents continue to opt to send their children to charter schools and their enrollments and waiting lists steadily increase. Why? One reason is that teachers in charter schools listen to and respect parents. They actively engage them in meaningful dialogue. They create partnerships. Even if the academic experience provided is no better than what is provided in the traditional public school, parents remain faithful to their charter school because they feel listened to, respected, and connected.

For too long, traditional public schools have not cultivated the same positive relationships with parents and the community. Until that changes, we will continue to see a flight to charter schools and private schools, as well as ongoing efforts to establish a voucher system that would dismantle public education as we know it. The choice is ours to make.

Creating A Shared Vision

To work successfully with parents, it is necessary to develop a shared vision of what we want. Remain focused on your shared goal: helping kids be more successful and productive. Although you may disagree about many things, this fundamental area of agreement is the foundation for building a successful alliance. With a shared goal, you can work through your differences. Without it, it is impossible to create a successful partnership.

From the outset, inspiring teachers are straightforward with parents about wanting all students to be successful and productive. They explain that this goal drives their behavior with students and parents. Once parents believe they share the same objective as the teachers, working collaboratively is relatively easy. Parents are less distrustful and suspicious and more supportive when they are confident that we are working toward the same goal. There may be disagreements about details, but those are easily managed once it is established that parents and teachers want the same thing.

A word of caution: Be mindful of how students perceive the connection between parents and teachers. It is not enough that kids see the adults working collaboratively. It is essential that they believe parents and teachers are working together for their benefit. If students believe that adults have joined forces against them, the results will be disastrous. Students will feel betrayed and powerless and will sabotage whatever parents and teachers do.

Tell Us About Your Child

We all want to be respected and feel that our opinions matter. When teachers ask for and use parent input, the relationship improves. Parents will be more supportive of teachers, and teachers will be more effective in the classroom. Ask parents how their children learn best and what strategies have been most successful in the past. A letter or questionnaire sent home at the beginning of the school year helps in this regard and lets the parents know you recognize their expertise.

It is also important to ask students for their input. How do they learn best? What strategies work best for them? Be certain to remind students that we learn in different ways and one of their jobs is to discover what learning strategies are most effective for them. This is an opportunity for students to gain power by taking responsibility for their learning, something inspiring teachers want for all students.

Parents Are Welcome

Many parents feel unwelcome in schools. They get the impression that teachers don't want to see them. These parents may disconnect and provide less academic support to their children. They may speak negatively about the school, teaching their kids that it is acceptable to treat teachers with disrespect. They almost assuredly will fail to support schools financially, reducing the resources available to their children.

Encourage parents to visit. In too many schools, the only time parents come is when there is a problem. In fact, some schools go so far as to ask parents to "shadow" their child for the day as punishment for poorly behaving students. That's the type of adult alliance to avoid. Instead, make classroom visits commonplace. When parents are a regular part of the landscape, their visits become less distracting. They fade into the background and students remain focused on their academic tasks.

Of course, classroom visitors can be a disruption. Some parents smother their children, providing so much assistance that the student has no opportunity to develop independence. Some parents become unnecessarily interested in situations that are none of their concern. Especially in secondary schools, where students need to develop independence and autonomy and separate from their parents, visits must be carefully orchestrated. Without clearly established parameters, parent visits can be counterproductive and significantly interfere with learning.

To prevent visits from being disruptive, develop clear and appropriate guidelines. Many find it useful to ask parents to assist in a very specific, defined task when they visit the classroom. This has several advantages. The students feel more comfortable when a visiting adult is helping instead of hovering. The parent feels useful when given something specific and constructive to do. It is also OK to tell parents that they can't visit on particular days or at certain times because it would compromise an activity. Parents need to schedule visits in a way that supports the educational experience.

Structured carefully and successfully, classroom visits will help parents better understand how hard teachers work as well as some of the demands involved in successful teaching. Parents who watch a skilled teacher work effectively with a classroom full of students become strong supporters of education.

Parent/Community Resources

Presentations by parents who are experts in particular fields can augment learning and strengthen teacher-parent relationships. It is more productive, inspiring, and meaningful for students to meet an archaeologist than to simply read about archeology. Let students and parents know that you would be delighted to have parent experts discuss topics being studied.

This type of presentation is different from what might take place on a "career day." While the latter can be a worthwhile way to get parents in the building, it is typically an isolated event with no connection to what is being studied. I am suggesting an invitation for parents to present when it is educationally relevant, not on a designated "career day."

Invite other experts from the community to speak to students as well. This builds a bridge between the school and the community and kids benefit by seeing what they learn in class being put into practice. Community members enjoy the opportunity, witness what takes place in an inspiring classroom, and see for themselves just how hardworking and effective teachers are. Community members who are actively involved with the school tend to be supportive and advocate for adequate school resources, including funding.

Volunteers

Relationships with the community are strengthened when teachers invite volunteers to assist in the classroom. Classroom volunteers are among teachers' most enthusiastic supporters. They know how hard teachers work and how challenging a job teaching can be. Because they appreciate what teachers do, they are advocates for the public support of education.

For a volunteer program to work effectively, it is critical for teachers to identify exactly what volunteers are being asked to do. Potential volunteers often shy away when the expectations are vague. They are uncomfortable not knowing what they will be asked to do and whether they have the skills to help. When recruiting volunteers, be specific about the assistance you need, the time commitment, and the skills required. Some schools provide training for volunteers. Given a clear picture of what is entailed, many hesitant parents become enthusiastic and helpful volunteers.

Summary

Inspiring teachers know that parents are a valuable resource. To create relationships that help more students be successful, they involve parents in the educational process. They seek parent input. They take steps to ensure that parents perceive the school as welcoming. They take advantage of parents' expertise to enhance student learning. They structure meaningful volunteer opportunities for parents. Parents who feel valued and respected develop a positive alliance with teachers, one that works for the benefit of the students.

Reflect, Personalize, & Implement

Reflect
- Identify some barriers to positive relationships with parents.
- What are some specific things you can do to develop a better working relationship with parents?
- What are some advantages of having positive relationships with parents?

Personalize
- What are some things you have done that have hampered the establishment of positive relationships with parents? What counterproductive behaviors have you observed in your colleagues?
- Do you think parents feel welcome and valued in your school? What specific things help and hinder your relationship with parents?
- Imagine you had a more positive relationship with parents. What impact would that have on student achievement? Job satisfaction?

Implement
- Identify three specific things you can do (individually and as a staff) to improve relationships with parents.
- What will you do to develop a shared vision with parents so that you are partners as opposed to potential adversaries?

CHAPTER 8

Conflict Management

When it comes to interpersonal relationships, conflict is inevitable. Even in the best of circumstances, there will be things you want that others don't, and things they want that you don't. There are times when we are driven by different quality world pictures. The only way to avoid conflict is to become a hermit.

Since we can never eliminate conflict, the reasonable goal is to manage it in a respectful, growth-enhancing way. Although the emphasis in this chapter is on managing conflict in a professional setting, the process is applicable to personal relationships as well.

Conflict does not need to be perceived negatively. In fact, when managed well, conflict facilitates our growth. Conflict invites us to move out of our comfort zone, giving us the opportunity to expand our horizons and broaden our knowledge and skills.

If you change your opinion after engaging in thoughtful dialogue, you have grown and profited. If your position remains unchanged, your ideas have been strengthened by withstanding argument and scrutiny and considering alternative points of view. Both outcomes are positive. It is interesting that many people resolutely avoid conflict when effective conflict management produces positive results regardless of where it leads.

Achieving Win/Win

The four potential outcomes of interpersonal conflict are:

- Win/Lose (Figure 8.1)

- Lose/Win (Figure 8.2)

- Kind of Win/Kind of Win (Figure 8.3)

- Win/Win. (Figure 8.4)

When we have a conflict, the behaviors that first pop into our head are those that meet the need for power, including "power over"" behaviors. In Win/Lose and Lose/Win (Figures 8.1 and 8.2), one party wins and the other loses. Most conflicts end with one of these unsatisfactory outcomes.

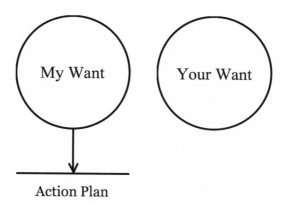

Figure 8.1: Win/Lose: You and I want different things. The action plan matches what I want. I win and you lose.

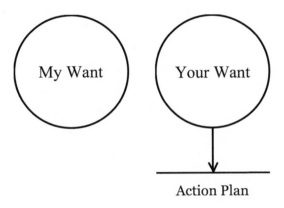

Figure 8.2: Lose/Win. You and I want different things. The action plan matches what you want. You win and I lose.

Ironically, in both these cases even the "winner" loses. Because I am driven by a need for belonging, which involves cooperating, I suffer if you lose. While my need for power is satisfied, my need to cooperate is frustrated. What some call "total victory" is not totally satisfying. Plus, because of the universal need for power, those who lose are often driven to "even the score," introducing a competitive element that may interfere with our ability to effectively collaborate. When the outcome produces winners and losers, the relationship becomes less need-satisfying and it is less likely we will produce quality work.

Until our definition of power includes "power with" – not just "power over" - and we have skills to manage conflict while maintaining a positive relationship, we will continue to engage in behaviors that inevitably lead to a winner and a loser. When we broaden our perception of power and consider long-term relationships, "power over" behaviors become less attractive. We seek solutions that result in achieving power without compromising personal relationships.

In "Kind of Win/Kind of Win," (Figure 8.3), our wants overlap, but there remains considerable discrepancy. The action plan is built on the area of agreement so each of us gets some of what we want. But since both of us fail to get all we want, we may feel as if we lost and our support of the action plan will be lukewarm at best.

"Kind of Win/Kind of Win" is the essence of negotiation and compromise. When negotiation and compromise are done without rancor and ill will, this is a satisfactory conflict resolution model. Unfortunately, that's the exception rather than the rule.

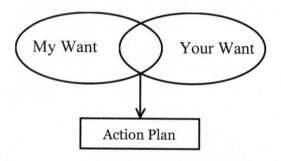

Figure 8.3: Kind of Win/Kind of Win

More frequently, people negotiate and compromise because they lack sufficient power to achieve a clear-cut win. Facing the prospect of a prolonged conflict, they reluctantly begin negotiating and compromising. In these circumstances, the goal is to get as much as possible while giving up as little as possible. There are still winners and losers, even if the victory and defeat are not as definitive. Those who get more of what they want and give up less feel like winners. Those who give up more are grateful for what they were able to salvage, but they still feel like losers.

Too often, negotiation and compromise is virtually indistinguishable from the Win/Lose and Lose/Win models. People feel less than satisfied and determined to get even the next time an opportunity presents itself. Ask anyone who has been involved in a labor dispute that was uncomfortably resolved by compromise. "Resolution" leaves participants unsatisfied and less trustful of one another. Working relationships are strained, if not permanently damaged. The Kind of Win/Kind of Win model may be preferable to those with clear-cut winners and losers, but the difference is often negligible.

Win/Win (Figure 8.4) is the only way to manage conflict that leaves all parties satisfied. In this model, when you and I realize that our wants don't match, we develop a new quality world picture that encompasses both what you want and what I want. Instead of negotiating – with each party trying to get the better deal – we create a vision that encompasses what both of us want. Because both of us end up with what we want, there is no compromise.

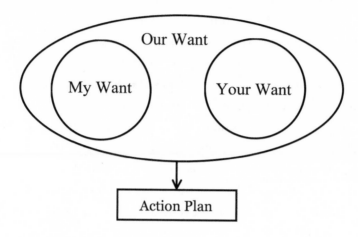

Figure 8.4: Win/Win. The action plan encompasses what each of us wants. Both of us feel like winners and support the plan with energy and enthusiasm.

Behind every quality world picture are underlying needs. For example, my want may meet my underlying need for recognition. As long as I get the recognition I need, I can give up my original want and embrace a new one. Because I still meet my needs, the solution represents a Win/Win situation.

It should be acknowledged that developing a shared quality world picture is sometimes impossible. What you want and what I want may be mutually exclusive, no matter how creative we are or how much we respect each other and work to resolve our conflict. Even then, it is still worth striving for the Win/Win ideal. This is no different from teachers pursuing the ideal that every student will do quality work nearly all the time. While no ideal is attained regularly – that's the nature of ideals – they are worth pursuing vigorously. If we are unable to create a Win/Win situation but have given it our best effort, we can gracefully move to negotiation and compromise without ill feelings and the outcome will be acceptable.

The conflict-management process is straightforward. First pursue a vision that encompasses what each party wants. If you are unable to achieve that ideal despite your best efforts, move to negotiation and compromise. While less than ideal, negotiation and compromise is successful when the parties treat one another respectfully and work to maintain the relationship. Done poorly and with hostility, negotiation and compromise can cause lasting damage. Finally, never resort to a process with clearly defined winners and losers. The cost is too high, even for those who appear to win.

Helping Others Resolve Conflict

There are times when you are not directly involved in a conflict but may be asked to mediate a dispute between others. As both a school psychologist and a middle school administrator, I often worked with students who were having difficulty getting along. The following conflict resolution process is adopted from the work of William Glasser (1998, 179). The example I provide illustrates the process with students, but it can be just as effectively used with adults.

1. Begin by saying the following: "I'd like to help you solve a problem you've been having. Are you here because you would like to resolve the problem?" It is essential to have each student affirm that they are seeking resolution. If either or both are unwilling to answer your question in the affirmative, the process stops. In my experience, virtually every student wants to resolve ongoing difficulties as long as they can maintain their power and dignity.

2. Each student is then asked the following: "Very briefly, what do you see as the problem?" I am clear with students about the guidelines. They are not to interrupt while the other is speaking. I inform students in advance that I may cut them off after thirty seconds or a minute. I only need a sense of what they see as the problem. The purpose here is to give kids a chance to be heard and to air their complaint. Typically, people cling to anger and conflict until they feel they have been heard, but I have no interest in spending unnecessary time on the problem. The goal is to resolve it.

3. At this point, ask each student, "Whose behavior can you control?" It is essential that each student verbally acknowledge that they are only able to control their own behavior. When we are involved in conflict, we typically try to control others. Because of the needs for autonomy and power, attempts to control others are universally resisted. I want students to take responsibility for their own behavior and understand they can only control their own actions.

4. The next question is often a challenge for students. Ask them, "What is one good quality about the other person?" Because they are having difficulty, they often balk at this question. I remind them that they indicated a desire to resolve the problem and that there must be some positive qualities about the other student or we wouldn't be having this conversation. Make sure that students know you are looking for personal characteristics. I often tell students, "I don't want to hear that she has really nice clothes or that he has a great smile. I'm interested in something about the person." This question frequently leads to an important

state change. I have seen students who were previously angry and hostile, begin to smile and make eye contact with each other as they say things like, "Well, he's really funny" or "She's always willing to help other kids who are having trouble." The importance of positive states was outlined in Chapter 2. This question helps kids transition to a state where they can resolve their difficulty.

5. Now that students are in a receptive state, say to each of them: "I need you to tell me one thing you will do in the next week to improve your relationship or solve the problem. This has to be something you will do *regardless of what the other person does*. I don't want to hear, 'I'll do this if...' This is something you need to promise no matter what the other person chooses to do." When a student offers something, I ask the other student if that would help because a gesture is only valuable if it is positively received.

6. I conclude by asking the students if they believe things will improve if they honor their commitments. I have used this process numerous times and students always affirm that this will help.

Students leave this process with several key learning points:

*   They affirm that they can only control their own behavior.

*   They realize that if they want a better relationship, they need to do something different.

- They learn that they can actively choose to solve problems instead of waiting passively for things to magically improve. This meets their need for power and competence.

- They learn that problems can be solved and relationships improved.

- They learn that taking responsibility instead of blaming others feels good and leads to success.

When Conflict Resolution Is Not An Option

Conflict resolution requires commitment from two or more people. Regardless of how effective any of us may be, we only control our own behavior, not that of others. If I want to resolve a conflict and you don't, there can be no resolution. When conflict resolution is not an option, it is helpful to cultivate behaviors that allow you to remain centered, calm, and accepting of what you can't control.

Remember that all people are doing the best they can. You can choose to perceive those unwilling to resolve conflict as simply doing what they know how to do instead of labeling them with disparaging terms like "pigheaded," "stubborn," and "petty." Which perception is more helpful? Which makes it easier for you to act like the person you want to be? Graciously accepting that the other does not yet have the capacity to rise above the conflict will help you stay centered and keep you from wasting energy on things out of your control.

Sometimes it is difficult to calmly accept another's behavior. When you find yourself stuck in an angry, hostile, or annoyed state, the following process will help. Begin by identifying your feelings about the other person and the labels you use (i.e. "pigheaded," "narrow minded," "spiteful," "condescending"). Are these labels accurate? How can you be certain that your chosen perception is correct? As you immerse yourself in this inquiry, you might discover that it is impossible to know conclusively that your chosen perception represents the truth, even if it seems valid.

The key to this process is asking yourself what benefit you receive from maintaining your negative perception of the other. Confront the truth that all behavior – including yours – is purposeful. There is no doubt whatsoever that you reap some benefit from perceiving the other person negatively. You may not want to admit it, but that negative perception is need-satisfying.

Whatever you get from your negative perception is important. Determine how to get the same benefit without resorting to the negative thoughts, feelings, and behaviors that prevent you from being the person you want to be. When you reach this point, your negativity will dissipate. It has served its purpose, assisting you until you created effective alternatives. This process keeps you in effective control of your life regardless of the choices made by those around you.

Summary

Conflict exists in every long-term relationship. Managed well, it leads to growth. Rather than fearing conflict, value it. Don't avoid or repress it, because conflict driven underground is impossible to manage successfully. View conflict as a sign that people are comfortable enough to make known what they want. Knowing that it offers an opportunity to achieve more quality in your life, approach conflict openly, honestly, and respectfully. Strive for a Win/Win outcome. If Win/Win is not possible, remain calm, centered, and focused regardless of how others behave.

Reflect Personalize, & Implement

Reflect

- Identify the following: "Win/Lose," "Lose Win," "Kind of Win/Kind of Win," "Win/Win."
- What is a possible negative outcome of negotiation and compromise?
- What can you do if "Win/Win" is unattainable?

Personalize

- What conflict management style do you typically use? Why?
- Are you ever in a position to help others resolve conflict? If so, how could you use the process outlined in this chapter?
- When you negotiate and compromise, are you still trying to "win"? Do you agree that negotiation and compromise is frequently an unsatisfactory process?

Implement

- What steps can you take to ensure that you strive for a "Win/Win" outcome when you face conflict?
- What specific steps can you take to maintain the positive relationships that foster high achievement when "Win/Win" is not attainable?

CHAPTER 9

Time Management

Being an inspiring teacher takes effort. Inspiring teachers continually update their learning plans, not satisfied using the same lessons year after year. They take advantage of worthwhile professional development opportunities, sharpening their skills and expanding their repertoire. Because staying fresh takes time, inspiring teachers need to develop time-management skills. Otherwise, they will burn out from stress and overwork. A strategy some teachers adopt is returning to a repetitive, less demanding teaching style. While withdrawing may help them survive, it does not allow them to become - or remain - inspiring teachers.

Teachers who implement the strategies presented in *The Inspiring Teacher* find their jobs easier to manage, in part because more responsibility is appropriately shifted toward students. When teachers define and regularly refer to the roles everyone in the class has identified and endorsed (see Chapter 5), there is more time to spend on important tasks and less squandered on peripheral, nonessential tasks.

Even though most teachers are busy, not all of them are busy doing what is most important. Inspiring teachers routinely ask, "Given my role and goal, is the task I'm doing appropriate and worth my time and energy?" Many traditional teachers spend considerable time doing chores that are not necessarily worth the effort.

Inspiring teachers decide where and how to invest their time and energy. They take control of their professional lives by acting professionally. Rather than acting on impulse or emotion, they consider their professional role and responsibilities, codes of ethical conduct, and district policy. With these important factors in mind, inspiring teachers identify where they have spent unproductive time, freeing them to do the more important work that inspires academic achievement and makes teaching the enriching experience it should be. Let's look at several areas where teachers can better utilize precious time.

Student Evaluation

Student evaluation is one area where many traditional teachers spend too much time. Inspiring teachers emphasize the importance of self-evaluation to students and provide them with skills to evaluate their own work in an honest, productive way. As a result, teachers avoid unnecessary correcting and students take more responsibility for improving their work before getting teacher feedback. If teachers improve only in this area, they will save countless hours while providing their students with an important skill that will serve them well throughout their lives.

Teaching students how to evaluate their own work takes time, but it is an investment that pays enormous dividends. Inspiring teachers develop meaningful rubrics with their students. They analyze models of quality work together.

I remember one classroom I visited where the teacher provided four models of student writing for her class to consider. The students had to identify the papers from 4 (the highest quality writing) to 1 (the lowest quality). Not surprisingly, the students had most difficulty deciding which model deserved a 2 and which model deserved a 3. The most impressive part of the class was the discussion the teacher facilitated where students identified the specific elements that determined whether a paper was a 1, 2, 3, or 4. They used their conversation to develop a rubric for the writing assignment they were about to begin and each student had a clear vision of what was needed to produce a high quality piece of writing. The discussion took about 30 minutes, inspired improved student writing, and saved the teacher hours in correcting.

By providing and developing rubrics and teaching the self-evaluation process, inspiring teachers help students improve their work without unnecessary teacher intervention. Students who have been given models and taught how to effectively self-evaluate become more responsible, independent learners. Teachers then have more time to do other things that make teaching enjoyable.

Don't Grade Everything

When I taught seventh-, eighth-, and ninth-grade English, grading writing assignments was enormously time-consuming. It was especially frustrating because my efforts made little impact. After I spent hours correcting papers, many students barely looked at my comments. I knew from other teachers that my experience was typical.

During my final two years as an English teacher, the school district put a heavy emphasis on student writing. Departmental guidelines required students to produce a certain amount of writing every week. The correcting that had been merely daunting quickly became overwhelming.

Sometimes our most creative and effective ideas emerge in desperate times. This was one of those occasions. Having decided it was impossible to read, correct, and comment on each piece of student writing, I developed a folder system (portfolios were not yet a common practice). Students put final drafts of each writing assignment in their folders. Periodically, I would say something like this to the students: "Each of you should now have six papers in your folder, three descriptive pieces and three persuasive pieces. Choose one paper that you want me to evaluate. I will then randomly choose two additional pieces, one persuasive and one descriptive. Make sure that what you have in your folder represents your best work and that you are ready to have it evaluated. All six papers should be in the folder when I collect it."

When I implemented this system, several things happened. First, because the students knew that anything in their folders might be evaluated, they began taking their assignments more seriously. I stopped hearing, "Is this going to be graded?" Second, because the students knew I would check that all assignments were completed, they didn't mind that I read only some pieces. They wanted credit for work they had done, but they didn't need specific feedback on every piece. Third, because students selected one paper to be graded, they carefully evaluated their work. They reviewed their papers and chose their best work. Since I graded their best work, they believed the system was fair. Giving them a choice also satisfied their need for freedom.

I had very few complaints. If students claimed they were "unlucky" because I had read some of their weaker pieces, I read more. The amount of reading and correcting I had to do, however, dropped significantly. Students wrote more and became better writers, while I had additional time to develop interesting, creative, and useful learning plans.

The Student-Centered Classrooms

Teachers save valuable time in student-centered classrooms. This type of classroom is characterized by more student activity and involvement than the traditional teacher-centered classroom. Inspiring teachers don't waste time putting together lengthy lectures and teacher-centered performances. Instead, they create an engaging environment that encourages all students to become active, fully involved participants in their own learning. With so many high-quality presentations available online, teachers can leave a lot of content delivery to someone else and make themselves available to facilitate student learning.

Brain research suggests students need time to make meaning from what has been presented in class. Inspiring teachers routinely have students interact with the content and with each other, reflect on their work, and process new information. With students actively engaged and independent, teachers have time to assist, coach, or provide individual assistance and remediation to those who need it. They are available to students for all the teachable moments that regularly occur in inspiring classrooms.

The Teacher As Facilitator

Inspiring teachers downplay their role as an expert and highlight their role as a facilitator. You don't need to know everything. Your primary goal is to excite students and get them on the road to discovery. Point students in the direction where information is available. This increases their independence and makes them more responsible for their own learning. Teachers don't need to be the source of all information.

Years ago, I was told that if a student asked a question and I didn't know the answer, I should say, "I don't know the answer, but I'll get back to you as soon as I can with the information." That kind of answer keeps the teacher in the role of information provider. It also perpetuates the notion that it is the teacher's job to do all the work. I encourage you to respond like this instead:

"That's an interesting question. Do you have any idea where you could find information to help you answer it? If not, maybe I can help you figure out where to look. When you've got some information, I'd be interested in hearing what you've learned. You can even share it with the rest of the class if it seems like a good idea."

This acknowledges the curiosity that many students bring to class, enables them to become experts and gain power responsibly in the classroom, and frees the teacher from having to dedicate precious time doing research the kids could be doing. The teacher is creating a community of learners, letting students contribute to the learning of the group.

"Get A Life!"

If you want to inspire others, begin by creating a well-balanced, satisfying life for yourself. Even the most dedicated teachers cannot inspire if they are unhappy.

Over the years, I watched too many teachers neglect their own needs, especially those for freedom and fun. Their passion for teaching and learning sustained them for a while, but eventually they burned out. Their lives were horribly unbalanced and ultimately unsatisfying. Focused exclusively on their role as teacher, they forgot that they needed time to relax, have fun, and socialize. Had they developed better time-management skills, they might have become happier – and better – teachers.

If you want to inspire your students, attend to your needs and manage your time so you can bring your energy, love of teaching, and happiness to the classroom.

Empowering & Employing Students

In many school systems, teachers are required to perform tasks that are incongruent with their training, expertise, and professional stature. They often cite chores like checking hall passes, signing students in and out of lavatories, and supervising students at lunch as a waste of their time and expertise. The irony is that many of those teachers who complain the loudest routinely undertake equally nonprofessional tasks in their own classrooms, frittering away time unnecessarily.

Before performing any task in the classrooms, ask, "Is this something I can appropriately delegate to the students?" If you can teach the students to perform the duty as well as you would, it will help them grow socially and/or academically. Relinquishing routine tasks to students provides you with additional time, increasing your effectiveness and enhancing your professionalism. Students feel a sense of power and responsibility when they get to do some of the chores that need to be undertaken for the classroom to function smoothly.

Effective Use Of Paraprofessionals

It's not uncommon for paraprofessionals (sometimes called classroom aides) and other support personnel to be woefully underused. They are often assigned mundane tasks, even though many are certified teachers and frequently have impressive teaching skills. Inspiring teachers use paraprofessionals effectively to give themselves more time.

In many cases, paraprofessionals would welcome the opportunity to contribute more significantly to the educational process. For example:

- Paraprofessionals can provide tutorial or remedial services to individual students or small groups. While some students require the expertise of a special needs teacher and specialized instruction, many learners thrive when paraprofessionals give them individualized attention in the regular classroom.

- Paraprofessionals can reduce the teacher's workload by correcting certain assignments. This and other time-consuming clerical tasks can easily be managed by someone other than the teacher. Paraprofessionals and teachers can also use technology to assist in many clerical tasks.

Of course, paraprofessionals should not be asked to do something for which they are unprepared or untrained. They often can, however, contribute more than they are currently asked or allowed to do.

Inspiring teachers develop supportive and effective working relationships with paraprofessionals. Most paraprofessionals who work with more than one teacher will say that they work harder and more enthusiastically for some teachers than for others. Ask them why, and they will use words such as "valued," "respected," and "useful." They appreciate being treated professionally and respectfully. When treated with dignity, most paraprofessionals provide tremendous support to teachers and help make the classroom a more productive learning environment.

Summary

It takes time and energy to become an inspiring teacher. Managing your workload more effectively will save you valuable time and make the journey easier. When students are taught how to evaluate their own work, they become more independent and responsible learners. Being judicious about assessing student work helps inspiring teachers safeguard their time. By structuring student-centered classrooms where teachers serve as facilitators and students are actively and independently involved in learning, teachers have time for students who require extra attention. Finally, inspiring teachers delegate appropriate classroom tasks to paraprofessionals and students. As inspiring teachers better manage their time, they free themselves to do the work that makes teaching a joyful experience.

Reflect, Personalize, & Implement

Reflect
- Why is important to develop effective time management skills?
- Identify some tasks that could be done by students or paraprofessionals that would save you time without compromising student achievement.

Personalize
- What effective strategies do you use to make more time for yourself?
- Would you be a more effective and more satisfied teacher if you managed your time better?
- Identify at least two areas where you spend time that would be better dedicated to more important educational tasks.
- If you continue to manage time as you do, are you likely to burn out?

Implement

- What will you do to make more time for yourself? Be specific. When will you begin?
- Identify how you can use students or paraprofessionals to lighten your workload so you can spend more time on more important tasks. When will you begin?

Final Thoughts

Do we make a difference? Absolutely. Every day. Whether we know it or not. The question to ask ourselves is: "What kind of difference do I want to make today in the lives of my students, their parents, my colleagues, and my profession?"

Here is an excerpt from an e-mail I received in September 2005: "A few days ago, I got an e-mail from someone that worked for me as an intern in the late 80s. His closing sentence was, 'You made a difference in my life, and I wanted you to know I appreciate it.' That got me thinking about people that had the same impact on me. You were the first person that I thought of. You challenged me not only to learn, but more importantly to think. So for what it's worth: you made a difference in my life and I wanted you to know I appreciate it."

David, the author of the e-mail I received, was a student in my ninth grade English class in Plymouth, Massachusetts, during the 1977-1978 school year. While I still recall him vividly today, I had no idea of my impact on him. I never saw him after that school year. It was more than 25 years later that I received his e-mail.

You, too, have made a difference in the lives of your students without ever realizing how influential you were. Caught up in our everyday routines, we forget how important we are to those we teach. *What we do matters.* Don't ever lose sight of that truth and the responsibility and promise it brings.

The inspiring classroom is a place like no other. It is where children grow into lifelong learners and critical thinkers who will make important contributions to our world. It is the place where genius is conceived. Every student deserves to be inspired by a passionate, caring, knowledgeable professional who brings the curriculum to life by making it meaningful, enjoyable, relevant, and vibrant.

But this isn't just about students. Kids aren't the only ones who are enriched in an inspiring classroom. Inspiring teachers, those who transform teaching from a job into a noble profession, receive as much as they give. Inspiring teachers make a difference in the world. Inspiring teachers touch the future.

Every one of you reading this book has the *capacity* to inspire. Your success will be determined by your *willingness* to inspire. If you are already on your way, I wish you continued success. If you are just beginning, the satisfaction that comes with knowing you are making a positive difference in the lives of children will be an exhilarating – and sometimes challenging - experience. Please don't settle for anything less.

Bibliography

Amabile, T. *Growing Up Creative.* NY: Crown, 1989.

Biehler, R. *Child Development: An Introduction.* 2d ed. Boston: Houghton Mifflin, 1981.

Boffey, B. *Reinventing Yourself: A Control Theory Approach to Becoming the Person You Want to Be.* Chapel Hill, N.: New View Publications, 1993.

Buck, N. *Peaceful Parenting.* San Diego, CA: Black Forest Press, 2000.

Burns, R. C. *Parents and Schools: From Visitors to Partners.* Washington, DC: The National Education Association, 1993.

Chapman, P. *If the Shoe Fits: How to Develop Multiple Intelligences in the Classroom.* Palatine, IL: Bantam Books, 1993.

Connors, K *Feeding the Brain.* NY: Plenum Press, 1989.

Covey, S. *The Seven Habits of Highly Effective People.* NY: Simon and Schuster, 1989.

Crawford, D., R. Bodine, and R. Hoglund. *The School for Quality Learning: Managing the School and Classroom the Deming Way.* Champaign, IL: Research Press, 1993.

Csikszentmihalyi, M. *Flow: The Psychology of Optimal Experience.* NY: HarperCollins, 1990.

Elkind, D. *Children and Adolescents: Interpretive Essays on Jean Piaget.* NY: Oxford University Press, 1970.

—*The Hurried Child: Growing Up Too Fast, Too Soon.* Reading, MA: Addison-Wesley, 1981.

—*All Grown Up and No Place to Go: Teenagers in Crisis.* Reading, MA: Addison-Wesley, 1984.

—*Miseducation: Preschoolers at Risk.* NY: Alfred A. Knopf, 1987.

Emerson, R.W. "The Divinity School Address."
http://www.harvardsquarelibrary.org/emerson_hds/

Erwin, J. *The Classroom of Choice: Giving Students What They Need and Getting What You Want.* Alexandria, VA: Association for Supervision and Curriculum Development, 2004.

Gandhi, M. Vol. 13, Ch. 153, page 241, 1913.
http://wiki.answers.com/Q/When_did_Gandhi_say_Be_the_change_you_want_to_see_in_the_world

Gardner, H. *Frames of Mind: The Theory of Multiple Intelligences.* NY: Basic Books, 1993.

----. *Intelligence Reframed. Multiple Intelligences for the 21st Century.* NY: Basic Books, 1999.

Gazziniga, M. *Mind Matters: How Mind and Brain Interact to Create Our Conscious Lives.* Boston, MA: Houghton Mifflin, in association with MIT Press, 1988.

Gilligan, Carol. *In a Different Voice: Psychological Theory and Women's Development.* Cambridge, MA: Harvard University Press, 1993.

Glasser, W. *The Quality School: Managing Students without Coercion.* NY: HarperCollins, 1990.

—. *The Quality School Teacher.* NY: HarperCollins, 1993.

—. Choice Theory: *A New Psychology of Personal Freedom.* NY: HarperCollins, 1998.

Gossen, D., and J. Anderson. *Creating the Conditions: Leadership for Quality Schools.* Chapel Hill, NC: New View Publications, 1995.

Greene, B. *New Paradigms for Creating Quality Schools.* Chapel Hill, NC: New View Publications, 1994.

Halpern, S. *Sound Health: The Music and Sounds That Make Us Whole.* San Francisco, CA: Harper and Row, 1985.

Howard, P. *The Owner's Manual for the Brain: Everyday Applications from Mind-Brain Research.* Austin, TX: Leornian Press, 1994.

How Difficult Can This Be?, produced and directed by Peter Rosen, 70 min, Peter Rosen Productions and PBS Video,1989, videocassette.

Jensen, E. *Brain-Based Learning and Teaching.* Del Mar, CA: Turning Point Publishing, 1995.

—.*Completing the Puzzle: The Brain-Based Approach.* Del Mar, CA: Turning Point Publishing, 1996.

—.*Teaching with the Brain in Mind.* Alexandria, VA: Association for Supervision and Curriculum Development, 1998.

__, *Different Brains, Different Learners: How to Reach the Hard to Reach.* Thousand Oaks, CA: Corwin Press, 2011.

Johnson, D. W., R. T. Johnson, and E. J. Holubec. *Circles of Learning: Cooperation in the Classroom.* 4th ed. Edina, MN: Interaction Book Co., 1993.

Kagan, S. *Cooperative Learning.* San Clemente, CA: Kagan Publishing, 1994.

Kegan, R. *The Evolving Self: Problem and Process in Human Development.* Cambridge, MA: Harvard University Press, 1982.

Kohn, A. *Punished by Rewards: The Trouble with Gold Stars, Incentive Plans, A's, Praise, and Other Bribes.* Boston, MA: Houghton Mifflin, 1993.

Leachman G., and Victor, D. (2003). "Student-Led Class Meetings." *Educational Leadership.* 60 (6), 64-68.

LeDoux, J. *The Emotional Brain: The Mysterious Underpinnings of Emotional Life.* NY: Simon and Schuster, 1996.

Lickona, T. *Raising Good Children: From Birth through the Teenage Years.* NY: Bantam Books, 1983.

Lozanov, G. "On Some Problems of the Anatomy, Physiology, and Biochemistry of Cerebral Activities in the Global-Artistic Approach in Modern Pedagogic Training." *Journal of the Society for Accelerative Learning and Teaching,* 16, 101-116,1991.

Ludwig, S., and K. Mentley. *Quality is the Key: Stories from Huntington Woods.* Wyoming, MI: KWM Educational Services, 1997.

Marzano, R. *A Different Kind of Classroom: Teaching with Dimensions of Learning.* Alexandria, VA: Association for Supervision and Curriculum Development, 1992.

Marzano, R and Marzano, J. (2003). "The Key to Classroom Management." *Educational Leadership.* 61 (1), 6-13.

Millman, D. *No Ordinary Moments: A Peaceful Warrior's Guide To Daily Life.* Tiburon, CA: H.J. Kramer, 1992.

National Education Association, *Building Parent Partnerships.* NEA Teacher-to-Teacher Books. Washington, DC: The National Education Association, 1996.

National Education Association, *Inclusive Classroom.* Washington, DC: National Education Association, 1998.

National Education Association, *Multiple Intelligences.* NEA Teacher-to-Teacher Books. 1996. Washington, DC: National Education Association.

National Education Association, *Time Strategies: Block Scheduling and Beyond.* NEA Teacher-to-Teacher Books. Washington, DC: The National Education Association, 1994.

Nunn, R. and J. Gallaher. *Inspiring Tranquility: Stress Management and Learning Styles in the Inclusive Classroom.* Washington, D.C.: National Education Association.

Ostrander, S. and L. Schroeder. *Super Memory.* NY: Carroll and Graf Publishers, 1991.

Peck, M. S. *The Different Drum: Community-Making and Peace.* NY: Touchstone, 1988.

Pink, Daniel. *Drive: The Surprising Truth About What Motivates Us.* New York, NY: Riverhead Books, 2009.

Powers, W. *Making Sense of Behavior: The Meaning of Control.* New Canaan, CT: Benchmark Publications, 1998.

Primason, R. *Choice Parenting: A More Connecting, Less Controlling Way to Manage Any Child Behavior Problem.* Lincoln, NE: iUniverse, Inc., 2004.

Rizzolatti, G, L.Fadiga, L. Fogassi, and V. Gallese. "Enhance: The Space Around Us." *Science,* 277: 190-191, 1997.

Rogers, S., J. Ludington, and S. Graham. *Motivation and Learning: A Teacher's Guide to Building Excitement for Learning and Igniting the Drive for Quality.* Evergreen, CO: Peak Learning Systems, 1997.

Rose, C. *Accelerated Learning.* NY: Dell, 1986.

Rozanski, A. "Mental Stress and the Induction of Silent Ischemia in Patients with Coronary Artery Disease." *New England Journal of Medicine* 318 (16): 1005-12, 1988.

Russell, P. *The Brain Book.* NY: Penguin Books, 1979.

Schacter, D. *Searching for Memory: The Brain, the Mind, and the Past.* NY: BasicBooks, 1996.

Schaps, E. "Creating a School Community." *Educational Leadership* 60 (6), 31-33, 2003.

Shea, J., M. Madden, and A. B. Shea. "Creating Your Own Homework." Plymouth, MA: Photocopy, 1997.

Sobo, EJ. (2012, August 7). "Schools & Self-Esteem, Or: Thank You for Making Those Socks!" *Huffington Post*: http://www.huffingtonpost.com/american-anthropological-association/school-and-self-esteem-or_b_1728969.html

Sparks, D & Hirsh, S. *A New Vision for Staff Development.* Alexandria, VA: Association for Supervision and Curriculum Development, 1997.

Sprenger, M. *Learning and Memory: The Brain in Action.* Alexandria, VA: Association for Supervision and Curriculum Development, 1999.

Sullo, R. *Teach Them to Be Happy.* Chapel Hill, NC: New View Publications, 1993.

—.*Inspiring Quality in Your School: From Theory to Practice.* Washington, DC: NEA Professional Library, 1997.

—.*Activating the Desire to Learn.* Alexandria, VA: Association for Supervision and Curriculum Development, 2007.

—.*The Motivated Student: Unlocking the Enthusiasm for Learning.* Alexandria, VA: Association for Supervision and Curriculum Development, 2009.

--- "Beyond Goals: Creating An Inspiring Classroom." http://www.funderstanding.com/gurus/beyond-goals-creating-an-inspiring-classroom/

Sylwester, R. *A Celebration of Neurons: An Educator's Guide to the Human Brain.* Alexandria, VA: Association for Supervision and Curriculum Development, 1995.

Tate, M. *"Sit and Get" Won't Grow Dendrites.* Thousand Oaks, CA: Corwin Press, 2004.

Thayer, R. *The Origin of Everyday Moods.* NY: Oxford University Press, 1996.

Tomlinson, C. *The Differentiated Classroom: Responding to the Needs of All Learners.* Alexandria, VA: Association for Supervision and Curriculum Development, 1999.

Westwater, A and P. Wolfe. "The Brain-Compatible Curriculum." *Educational Leadership*, 58(3), 49-52, 2000.

Wonder, Stevie. *I Wish.* 1976. http://en.wikipedia.org/wiki/I_Wish_(Stevie_Wonder_song)

Wubbolding, R. *Using Reality Therapy.* NY: HarperCollins, 1988.

Wolfe, P. *Brain Matters: Translating Research into Classroom Practice.* Alexandria, VA: Association for Supervision and Curriculum Development, 2001.

Suggested Web Sites

The following sites provide useful information and links to other valuable sites.

- ASCD: www.ascd.org
- Bob Sullo: www.internalmotivation.net
- Jensen Learning Corporation: www.jlcbrain.com
- National Education Association: www.nea.org
- The William Glasser Institute: www.wglasser.com
- William Glasser International: http://www.wglasserinternational.org
- Choice Theory Resources: http://effectivecontrol.net
- Peaceful Parenting: http://www.peacefulparenting.com
- The Generative Leadership Project: http://genleadership.com
- Bette Blance & Associates: http://betteblance.com
- Doug Dragster: https://www.facebook.com/dougdragster
- Inspiration for Education: http://www.inspiringmotivation.com
- Alfie Kohn: http://www.alfiekohn.org
- Collaborative for Academic, Social, & Emotional Learning: http://casel.org
- The Institute for Habits of Mind: http://www.instituteforhabitsofmind.com
- Edutopia: http://www.edutopia.org
- ASCD Whole Child Initiative: http://www.wholechildeducation.org
- Centered in Choice: http://www.centredinchoice.com/
- Caine Learning: http://www.cainelearning.com
- Funderstanding: http://www.Funderstanding.com

About the Author

An educator for nearly forty years, Bob Sullo has been an English teacher, adjustment counselor, school psychologist, and middle school administrator. Over the course of his career, he has worked with both regular education and special education students from pre-K through graduation in elementary, middle, and high school. A senior faculty member of William Glasser International, Bob now conducts staff development sessions on a full-time basis and has provided workshops to educators and parents in the United States, Canada, South America, Europe, Australia, and New Zealand. His sessions highlight internal control, internal motivation, personal responsibility, and the importance of inspiring students to be academically productive in a joyful environment.

In addition to *The Inspiring Teacher: Making A Positive Difference In Students' Lives,* Bob is the author of *Teach Them To Be Happy* (New View Publications, 1993), *Inspiring Quality in Your School* (NEA Professional Library, 1997), *Activating the Desire to Learn* (ASCD, 2007), *Managing to Inspire: Bringing Out the Best in Those You Supervise* (iUniverse, 2007), and *The Motivated Student* (ASCD, 2009).

Bob and his wife live in Sandwich, Massachusetts. For workshops, keynotes, or other presentations, contact Bob at:

E-mail: bob@internalmotivation.net
Website: www.internalmotivation.net

Other Books by Bob Sullo

Teach Them To Be Happy

Inspiring Quality In Your School: From Theory To Practice

Activating The Desire To Learn

Managing To Inspire: Bringing Out The Best In Those You Supervise

The Motivated Student: Unlocking The Enthusiasm For Learning

See Bob's Amazon Author page for links to all his books.

Ever wish kids were more motivated? If you're like most of us, you have tried rewards and punishments to motivate kids. There's only one problem: they don't work. At least not well enough.

It's time to challenge the status quo and create schools, classrooms, and homes based on what really motivates behavior.

Are you ready to move beyond the reward/punishment model and embrace a whole new way to understand motivation?

For information about Bob's books and to learn how to make school a productive, joyful place for kids and teachers, visit www.internalmotivation.net.

About the Publisher

Funderstanding was founded 20 years ago out of pure, unmitigated frustration. Frustration that our school system was failing our children. Anger that learning had been replaced by memorization and regurgitation. Disappointment at watching our kids put through drill-and-kill exercises with no consideration for their individual strengths and weaknesses, or even their interests.

Out of all this negative emotion emerged a positive idea. When fun intersects with understanding, education *can* be inspired. Our kids *can* look forward to learning and revel in those amazing "gee whiz" moments. It takes work, but it's worth it.

Visit us at Funderstanding.com.